A • B G C • M O N O G R ^ ᴾ H

D0861096

Renewal
in
Theological
Education

◆

STRATEGIES
FOR
CHANGE

R O B E R T W. F E R R I S

Renewal in Theological Education

Strategies for Change

ISBN 1-879089-03-3

Table of Contents

Appendices

Tables and Figures

Abbreviations Used

AABC	American Association of Bible Colleges
ACTEA	Accrediting Council for Theological Education in Africa
ALET	Asociacion Latino-americano de Educacion Teologica
ANCC	All Nations Christian College
APCTE	Association for Promotion of Chinese Theological Education
ATA	Asia Theological Association
ATS	Association of Theological Schools
BGC	Billy Graham Center, Wheaton, IL USA
CBC	Canadian Bible College
C&MA	Christian and Missionary Alliance
CBCS	Columbia Bible College and Seminary
CBSE	Conservative Baptist Seminary of the East
CETA	Caribbean Evangelical Theological Association
CGST	China Graduate School of Theology
CSBE	Columbia School of Biblical Education
CTS	Canadian Theological Seminary
ECWA	Evangelical Churches of West Africa
EETA	European Evangelical Theological Association
ICAA	International Council of Accrediting Agencies for Evangelical Theological Education
JETS	Jos ECWA Theological Seminary
PABATS	Philippine Association of Bible and Theological Schools
PAFTEE	Philippine Association for Theological Education by Extension
SPABC	South Pacific Association of Bible Colleges
TAFTEE	The Association for Theological Education by Extension
TAP	Theological Assistance Program of WEF
TEE	Theological Education by Extension
TEF	Theological Education Fund
UBS	Union Biblical Seminary
WEF	World Evangelical Fellowship

INTRODUCTION

It strikes me as foolish to pretend that a manuscript such as this arises without historical roots or emotional commitment. Since the truth is quite the opposite, I believe the reader will be better equipped to assess the pages which follow if I share a bit of myself.

My first interest in Christian missions and the Church of Jesus Christ worldwide developed during early teenage years when my parents served as missionaries in Liberia, West Africa. Years later, when I was a student at Wheaton College, that interest took more specific form as I recognized God's call to theological education overseas. I thank God for my early exposure to the challenges (and blessings!) of work in the Two-Thirds World and for the influence of disciplined and godly instructors in college, graduate school, and seminary.

In 1967 my wife and I went to the Republic of the Philippines for a ministry in theological education under SEND International (then Far Eastern Gospel Crusade). After initial language and culture learning, I was assigned to teach theology and New Testament at FEBIAS College of Bible near Manila. From the outset I was a teacher in search of better ways of helping students learn.

When theological education by extension (TEE) first came to the Philippines in 1972, I was not interested. I told friends that I just wanted to be the best classroom teacher God had enabled me to be. One day a colleague commented that enrolling for a TEE writers workshop would make me a better classroom teacher, and I was hooked. In TEE I found a community of kindred spirits, all searching for more effective ways to train church leaders for ministry. Within three months of that workshop I was elected to the board of Philippine Association For Theological Education by Extension (PAFTEE), and eighteen months later I was appointed PAFTEE's Executive Director.

As a result of my service with PAFTEE, I came to recognize that a theological educator must be a dual professional—it is not enough to be a theologian, one also must be an educator. In the Philippines, furthermore, the challenges that boggled us were not theological problems; we knew how to solve those. The problems we could not solve were educational. I determined then that I would seek the training needed to address those problems. My mission granted a study leave, and I enrolled in a program on educational curriculum and administration.

Two years later I returned to the Philippines to resume my appointment with PAFTEE and, within a few months, to add a concurrent appointment as Executive Director of Philippine Association of Bible and Theological Schools (PABATS). The next four years were filled with challenges and blessings as I was repeatedly forced to clarify my own educational values and articulate the meaning of those values in concrete settings. Theological educators in the Philippines work with very modest resources, but they are deeply committed to the truth of Scripture and to their calling to serve the Church. They often amazed me with their openness to adapt training strategies and structures in order to more effectively equip church leaders.

During those years I became aware of the International Council of Accrediting Agencies for Evangelical Theological Education (ICAA). Although I did not attend the Council's meetings in 1980 and 1981 (I had no budget), I was invited to comment on issues before the Council, including early drafts of a project known as "A Manifesto on the Renewal of Evangelical Theological Education" (see Appendix A). I was delighted by the spirit represented in the "Manifesto" and was happy to contribute to its formulation. When invited to present papers at ICAA consultations held in 1984 and 1987,[1] I seized each occasion as an opportunity to press the urgency of the renewal agenda outlined in the "Manifesto."

Prior to the 1987 ICAA Consultation on "Excellence and Renewal in Theological Education," I had been nominated by SEND International as Billy Graham Center (BGC) Missionary Scholar in Residence. Although I had filed most of the qualifying papers, however, I had not settled on a research project to propose to Graham Center administrators.

During the consultation I conceived a project which would examine the context for renewal in evangelical theological education and explore the impact of the ICAA "Manifesto on the Renewal of Evangelical Theological Education" adopted four years before. At the closing business session of those meetings I explained my research interest and was granted qualified endorsement by ICAA to submit a formal proposal to the Billy Graham Center. To the delight of many, the proposal was selected for the 1988-89 Missionary Scholar In Residence appointment. The project proposed would consist of four parts:

1. Clarification of the meaning of "renewal" as advocated in the ICAA "Manifesto."
2. Identification of evangelical theological schools which demonstrate values advocated in the ICAA "Manifesto."
3. Survey of ways the ICAA Manifesto has been used to promote renewal values in theological education.
4. Development of guidelines for implementing a program of renewal in existing theological education institutions.

With the enormous assistance of friends and the facilities of the Billy Graham Center at Wheaton College, the project was completed as proposed. The resources of the Graham Center Library very adequately supported the historical and theoretical aspects of the research. Reams of questionnaires were printed and distributed, and responses tallied and analyzed. All this was attended by a constant flow of correspondence and telephone conferences.

Without doubt, the most encouraging—and stimulating—aspect of this study has been the opportunity to visit schools around the world which have taken deliberate and positive strides toward renewal of theological education. Overall, these schools are rare, but they do exist. On the basis of survey responses and conversations with knowledgeable theological educators, ten schools were identified which illustrate this phenomenon.[2] These schools are not alone; it would be easy (and very profitable) to add ten more. The schools selected, however, were:

Conservative Baptist Seminary of the East, Dresher, Pennsylvania
Columbia Bible College and Seminary, Columbia, South Carolina
Canadian Theological Seminary, Regina, Saskatchewan
All Nations Christian College, Ware, Hertfordshire, England
Bibelschule Brake, Lemgo, Federal Republic of Germany
Jos ECWA Theological Seminary, Jos, Plateau State, Nigeria
Union Biblical Seminary, Pune, Maharashtra State, India
China Graduate School of Theology, Kowloon Tong, Hong Kong
Bible College of South Australia, Adelaide, South Australia
Tahlee Bible College, Karuah, New South Wales, Australia

Between the first of January and the end of April, 1989, I visited these institutions. My intention was to spend at least four days on each campus. In that time, I found I could identify those aspects of training which are most creative and demonstrative of renewal values, and I could explore the factors which contributed to development of these innovations. While on campus, I drafted a case study which described the programs or qualities of interest, and the factors contributing to their development. Before leaving campus I requested the president or principal to review the case study, providing correction or adding detail as necessary.[3] I am deeply indebted to the administration and faculty of each institution for the high level of cooperation—often sacrificial—which was accorded me.

From the outset I was asked to clarify what I mean by "renewal of evangelical theological education." The choice of the term is problematic, since it is easily confused with "church renewal"—a very distinct (and quite different) concept.[4]

The easiest response is to point the questioner to the ICAA "Manifesto" since I believe the values articulated there provide an adequate catalog of the goals I seek. I embrace these values solely because I recognize them as biblically valid and educationally appropriate. The same conviction motivates my efforts to help theological educators realize those values in their institutions.

The plan of the book moves from history, to need, to examples, to implications. Some readers may want to bypass the historical and research materials, Chapters 1 to 3, and go directly to the case studies. They are encouraged to do so. Others, however, will find the historical background alerts them to common factors at work in the cases reported. The research data, furthermore, assures readers that their own desire for renewal is broadly shared.

I owe a considerable debt of gratitude to the many who have made this study possible. First mention must be made of the board and staff of the Billy Graham Center at Wheaton College. Their commitment to ministry training is a function of their larger commitment to extending and developing the Church of Jesus Christ worldwide. SEND International supported my commitment to renewal of theological education during twenty-one years of ministry in Asia, as well as my year at the Billy Graham Center. This project also could not have been accomplished without the support and encouragement of the board and officers of ICAA, especially the Executive Secretary, Robert Youngblood, and Board Chairman Randall Bell.

Special mention also must be made of several individuals at the Billy Graham Center. James Kraakevik, BGC Director, proved to be a kind friend and supportive supervisor. Jane Nelson, Director of Scholarship Programs, processed my application, supervised appointment of a guidance committee, and encouraged me throughout my project. Dotsey Welliver provided excellent editorial counsel. Dan Moul assisted with processing statistical data. Jenny Dowdy and Marilyn Weissing looked out for me and made sure I had everything I needed to carry out my work.

My advisory committee included James Kraakevik, Merrill Ewert, Eugene Gibbs, Melvin Lorentzen, Lois McKinney, Jane Nelson, Wilbert Norton, and Timothy Phillips. These men and women, individually and as a group, wisely advised and faithfully encouraged me throughout the project.

I am very thankful, as well, for the support I receive from my wife, Sue, and from our children, Rosalyn and Roger. Most of all, however, our family praises God for the privilege of being part of his gracious work of equipping leaders for the Church around the world.

CHAPTER 1

Renewal Of Theological Education: The Larger Picture

A recent seminary graduate fights discouragement daily as he struggles with an increasingly ineffective ministry in the suburban church he pastors.

In a nearby community, a young fellow-minister has already succumbed to pastoral stress and abandoned the ministry for a secular job.

Both of these sincere and dedicated young men help illustrate the state of current theological education. Observers in the field today commonly employ language of concern—sometimes alarm—when discussing the situation. Seminaries are "directionless," faculties are "competitive," curricula are "unrelated to life," and graduates are "ill prepared for ministry." To be sure, occasional voices are raised in defense of the received programs of ministry preparation, but they are often drowned by the dissatisfied and the restless.

Both positions can be argued from evidence. In many parts of the world the graduates of Bible colleges and seminaries serve the church with distinction. At the same time, a majority of their classmates struggle in unproductive ministries or have abandoned their pulpits for the marketplace.

This situation is not new, nor is the rising chorus calling for "reform" or "renewal" of theological education. Indeed, a great deal of attention (and funding) has been devoted during this century to the apparent malaise of theological education.

The Association of Theological Schools And Renewal of Theological Education in North America

In North America, efforts toward evaluation and redirection of theological education have formed a sub-theme for the programs of the Association of Theological Schools in the United States and Canada (ATS). On three occasions, furthermore, large grants have been obtained for critical appraisal of theological education in North America.

In the early 1930s, John D. Rockefeller, Jr., funded a study directed by William Adams Brown of Union Theological Seminary. Brown and his colleagues charted the proliferation of subjects in theological curricula and concluded that the curriculum must be dictated by the practice of ministry rather than the explosion of research interests. When pressed to describe what that means, however, they provided no guidelines for implementing their observations.

Twenty years later the Carnegie Corporation provided a major grant to staff and underwrite a center for the Study of Theological Education in the United States and Canada. The study team, led by H. Richard Niebuhr, visited more than ninety North American Protestant seminaries and studied reports and statistical information from every institution affiliated with the American Association of Theological Schools (the former name of the ATS), and many others besides. Niebuhr and his colleagues suggested that the concepts of "priest," "preacher," and "evangelist" are no longer helpful, but that seminaries should design programs which develop "pastoral directors." The team further suggested that the quest for integration in theological education can be realized only in a student's ability to arrive at "personal synthesis," and only if the faculty consists of a genuine *collegium* of teachers who have not only achieved personal synthesis for themselves, but also realize as a group of intellectual workers the unity of the Church. (Niebuhr, et al., p. 83.)

Despite the considerable investment of resources and talent, neither the 1930s study led by Brown nor the 1950s study led by Niebuhr have had a discernible impact on the practice of training for ministry.

Recently the Association of Theological Schools has obtained another major grant, this time from the Lilly Endowment, to support "a multifaceted study of theological education." Although the program is continuing, two books which have emerged from the project are Hough and Cobb's *Christian Identity and Theological Education* (1985), and Stackhouse's *Apologia: Contextualization, Globalization, and Mission in Theological Education* (1988). Sadly, both titles are more useful for documenting the distressing state of North American theological education than for pointing the way toward equipping Church leaders.

The International Missionary Movement
And Renewal of Theological Education Worldwide

Parallel to the ATS studies (and, at times, intersecting with them), the international missionary movement has provided a second and more productive impetus toward renewal of theological education. Although evident earlier (cf. Lienemann-Perrin, pp 1-7), the need and call for renewal was sounded with dramatic clarity at the International Missionary Council's 1938 conference in Tambaram, Madras, India.

Almost all the younger churches are dissatisfied with the present system of training for the ministry and with its results. In many reports received from different parts of the world, it is stated that there are ministers of a poor standard of education, who are unable to win the respect of the laity and to lead the churches, that some are out of touch with the realities of life and the needs of their people, and are not distinguished by zeal for Christian service in the community. (International Missionary Council, pp. 188-189.)

Section VIII of the Madras Meetings, addressing "The Indigenous Ministry of the Church, Both Ordained and Lay," concluded its report with a plea for more careful attention to the task of ministry preparation.

It is our conviction that the present condition of theological education is one of the greatest weaknesses in the whole Christian enterprise, and that no great improvement can be expected until churches and mission boards pay far greater attention to this work, particularly to the need for cooperative and united effort, and contribute more largely in funds and in personnel in order that it may be effectively carried out.

In writing this report, we have used all the material submitted to us, but we are conscious that it has been prepared on the basis of very inadequate information. We think that the time has come for a much more thorough investigation and survey of this field than has as yet been carried out. Valiant experiments are being made, and new methods are being tried in different countries. But these enterprises are for the most part isolated, and there is hardly any exchange of experience and ideas between the different areas.

We, therefore, instruct the Committee of the International Missionary Council to take action in this matter, in consultation with the churches, and that a commission be appointed as soon as possible, to arrange for the preparation of detailed studies of the situation, where these have not already been made, to visit the main centers of theological education and to work out a policy and program for the training of the ministry in the younger churches. (International Missionary Council, pp 198-199.)

Almost before these words could be published, the world was engulfed in war. The National Christian Council of India, Burma, and Ceylon determined to proceed with a study of its own, recognizing that the war would impose inevitable delays in any international response. In 1945, Charles Ranson, Secretary of the National Christian Council, published *The Christian Minister in India: His Vocation and Training*. Ranson's report was the first "detailed study" prepared in response to the Tambaram call.

With the conclusion of the war, the International Missionary Council resumed the task of reviewing ministry preparation. Four reports of varying scope were produced before the task was overtaken by new initiatives. Between 1950 and 1954, a three-part report was compiled, titled *Survey of the Training of the Ministry in Africa* (Neill, 1950; Bates, et al, 1954; and Goodall and Nielsen, 1954). In 1956 Ranson was recruited to direct a *Survey of the Training of the Ministry in Madagascar*. The International Missionary Council merged with the World Council of Churches, Commission on World Mission and Evangelism, in 1960, but the work continued. Webster's *Survey of the Training of the Ministry in the Middle East* and Scopes' *The Christian Ministry in Latin America and the Caribbean* were published by the WCC in 1962. By documenting the vast need for ministry training in the developing world, these studies gave rise to establishment of the Theological Education Fund in 1958.

Although the Theological Education Fund (TEF) owed its origin to the call issued at Tambaram, it seemed unaware of the dissatisfaction with traditional ministry education expressed at that conference. Furthermore, missionary theological educators were apparently oblivious of the "dis-ease" in North American seminaries, documented by the ATS studies.

When the Theological Education Fund was founded in 1958, throughout the world there was much less uncertainty about what constituted "good" theological education than today. There was wide consensus that the national churches of the Third World could best raise their standards of ministerial training by duplicating, as best they could within their own cultural settings, the patterns of the Western theological seminaries. To do this it was clear what was required: the development of B.D. and postgraduate programmes within ecumenical and, if possible, university settings; the support of regional accreditation programmes to stimulate and regulate academic standards; the provision of adequate buildings, libraries, and textbooks; and the training of national staff members on post-graduate levels who would then be equipped to administer and teach. (Bergquist, p. 244.)

So it was that TEF's "First Mandate Period" (1958-1964) sought to promote academic excellence through three programs. One provided major grants of $100,000 or more to twenty-seven selected theological schools in Africa, Asia, and Latin America, a second provided funds for library development at nearly 300 theological schools in the Third World, and the third established about twenty-five vernacular textbook programs for writing, translating, and publishing theological texts. Shoki Coe, TEF's third director, later wrote:

For me, as an Asian theological educator, the word "advance" summed up the call of the First Mandate. It was as fascinating to us out there as the word "development" in more recent years. But the direction of our advance was not called into question. (Coe, p. 234.)

If the word "advance" characterized the First Mandate period, then Coe suggests "rethink" captures the mood of the Second Mandate (1965-1969). Using a pen name, C. Hwang, Coe wrote a paper in 1962, titled "A Rethinking of Theological Training for the Ministry in the Younger Churches Today" (Hwang: 1962), which set the tone for TEF programs under the Second Mandate. The textbook and library development programs were continued, as well as support for regional associations of theological schools. More than 400 scholarships were also granted to enable Third World nationals to pursue advanced study in the West. The central agendum of the Second Mandate is reflected, however, in the Director's report to a 1967 meeting of the TEF Committee.

It was once said that the second phase of the TEF was given to create a crisis in Younger Church theological education, an occasion in which the financial barriers to a creative rethinking of the theological task would be so effectively and dramatically removed that the course of ministerial training would be decisively altered. This has not yet occurred. (Cited in Lienemann-Perrin, pp 137-138.)

Nor did it.

This was not a consequence of wrong guidelines, for it was precisely the relevance of ministerial training which the TEF had made the major criterion for its strategy in the Second Mandate. However, neither the TEF nor its working partners in the First and Third World had recognized or taken seriously enough the radical consequences of these guidelines. (Lienemann-Perrin, p. 138.)

Instead of being invested in projects to promote renewal, the TEF money was used to support small local projects and "unimportant, internal matters."

No doubt the frustration of this experience dictated "reform" as the theme of the Third Mandate period (1970-1977). At the outset of that period, TEF's second director died, and Taiwanese theologian Shoki Coe was appointed to assume leadership of TEF. Commenting on the mandate that faced him, Coe notes:

The search for renewal in theological education had reached the most critical point. We were driven to ask the basic questions: What is theological education? What is it for—not in abstraction but in the setting of the contemporary, revolutionary world, and especially of the Third World which was undergoing drastic changes and crying out for justice and liberation? (Coe, p. 237.)

Coe and his colleagues at TEF responded to this challenge with two interrelated concepts. The first Coe termed "double wrestle."

By [these words] I mean wrestling with the Text from which all texts are derived and to which they point, in order to be faithful to it in the context; and wrestling with the context in which the reality of the Text is at work, in order to be relevant to it. (Coe, p. 238.)

The second term, "contextualization," became the central focus of the Third Mandate period. Again, Coe defines his term:

So in using the word *contextualization*, we try to convey all that is implied in the familiar term *indigenization*, yet seek to press beyond for a more dynamic concept which is open to change and which is also future oriented. (Coe, p. 241.)

The immense significance of this concept gripped Coe and his colleagues at TEF. They saw contextualizing, first of all, as a measure of the crisis facing the Church and its educational agencies (cf. Bergquist). They also saw it as a task and the methodology by which the task is pursued. This led Coe to comment, "I am convinced we have come upon something vital for the renewal of theological education" (Coe, p. 240). One may be reluctant to endorse the assumptions behind that conclusion (cf. Conn), but there is no doubt that TEF's focus on contextualization of theology and ministry provided powerful impetus for renewal of theological education.

Theological Education by Extension: A Renewal Movement Gone Astray

In contrast to the ample resources available to the Association of Theological Schools and the Theological Education Fund, theological education by extension (TEE) originated in a failing seminary in a small Central American country. The origins and early history of TEE are well documented (Winter; Covell and Wagner), although certain details are obscured by the breathless tones in which the story is told.

It is worth noting that the faculty of the Presbyterian Seminary in Guatemala did not set out to develop an alternative model of theological education. In 1962 they were faced with a desperate situation in their church and in their seminary; they knew they had to do something. The pattern of training which came to be known as TEE evolved through a series of *ad hoc* experiments aimed at improving the effectiveness of the Seminary. It is not inaccurate, therefore, to say that TEE had its origin in one seminary's quest for renewal of theological education.

Although the faculty of the Presbyterian Seminary in Guatemala was excited about the response of students to their innovations, it is doubtful that they recognized the significance others would soon attribute to their efforts. The first breakthrough came in "a chance conversation with Dr. James Hopewell who was then the associate director of the T.E.F." when the experiment was less than a year old (Winter, p. 22). Hopewell encouraged the faculty, provided an important contact for a TEF grant to the Seminary, and later commended their program in the *International Review of Missions* (Winter, p. 36).

To this point the experimental program of training had received attention primarily from the TEF and the World Council of Churches Division of World Missions and Evangelism. In July 1966, however, the faculty of the Presbyterian Seminary reported their experiment at a

workshop sponsored by the Committee to Assist Ministry Education
Overseas (CAMEO) held at the Central American Mission Bible Institute in Guatemala City. The evangelical Bible institute educators were
immediately attracted to the concept of extension training and left the
workshop with great excitement. Two months later the faculty ran a one
week workshop on "The Extension Seminary and the Programmed
Textbook" in Armenia, Columbia, under the sponsorship of Asociacion
Latino-americano de Educacion Teologica (ALET). The workshop received wide publicity in the conciliar and evangelical press and piqued
the attention of theological educators worldwide. This led to a CAMEO
sponsored "Seminary Extension Workshop," held December 19-21,
1968, in Wheaton, Illinois, and attended by 120 missionaries and mission
executives from around the world. The enthusiastic response to this
workshop set in motion plans for CAMEO to duplicate the workshop in
Africa and Asia in 1970.

During its Third Mandate period (1970-1977), the TEF added a focus
on innovations in theological education. Initially this took the form of
additional support for experiments in theological education by extension. TEF administrators became increasingly concerned, however, that
TEE was employed as an instrument of indoctrination rather than
liberation. After 1973, the TEF shifted its attention and support to
experiments in dialogical learning, modeled on Paulo Freire's program
for literacy and "conscientization" in Brazil.

At some point in TEE's meteoric ascent to world acclaim, the
innovation became a movement and, in the process, acquired an aura of
myth. Although motives clearly were high and no deception was
intended, much that was aspiration in the Guatemalan experiment was
assumed to be fact, and held up for the emulation of others. Even more
subtly, descriptive accounting of one institution's innovations was
transmuted into prescriptive instruction on how ministry training
ought to be done. Programmed instructional texts and frequent (i.e.,
weekly) center meetings led by lay "facilitators" ("the text is the
teacher") constituted the essential components of the TEE program.
TEE became a stylized "alternative model" of ministry training in
competition with a more established, traditional—and equally stylized—
"residential" model.

Tragically, the case for TEE was argued with great vehemence,
almost always by contrasting the strengths of TEE with "inappropriate"
and "ineffective" patterns of "residential" seminaries. As a result, the
debate was polarized, and what began as a promising adventure in
renewal of theological education was reduced to a sectarian debate.

It would be a mistake to conclude that the energies expended on TEE were wasted. Through TEE, thousands—perhaps hundreds of thousands—of Christians in the "Third World" have received ministry training which otherwise would have been inaccessible to them. Just as important, theological educators have been confronted with educational issues and have been exposed to basic principles of adult education. Even the TEE "residence seminary" debate had some redeeming value in that it highlighted issues which demand the attention of theological educators. The mere realization that there is more than one way to train for ministry has been an eye-opening experience for some.

Although TEE literature rarely mentions renewal of theological education, the effect of TEE has been to focus dissatisfaction with present patterns of training for ministry and nourish the hope that more effective strategies exist. To that extent, at least, it must be viewed as contributing to the present context for renewal.

Recent Voices Calling for Renewal

Alongside the sources of impetus for renewal already considered, several individuals have appealed to theological educators to reconsider the goals and procedures of their training programs. In January, 1978, Anglican Bishop Lesslie Newbigin addressed a conference of theological college teachers from his communion with a paper titled, "Theological Education in a World Perspective." Newbigin used the experience of the TEF as a point of departure to challenge British theological educators to reconsider the structure of the ministry, methods of ministerial formation, and the content of theological study. He asks probing questions and suggests thought-provoking responses.

Must we not face the fact in this country also that the model of ministry as a full-time salaried professional group, analogous to the doctors and the lawyers, is a legacy from a period of history which has now passed? We know, in fact, that it has already broken down.... Would it not be in accordance both with Scripture and with our real situation if (at least in many of our scattered parishes) it was a local and respected elder of the local congregation who normally presided at the Eucharist, and a full-time salaried person who would be his auxiliary both to supplement his teaching ministry and also to assist him in the continuing process of leadership-development? (Newbigin, p. 6.)

Newbigin asserts that "true theology can be done only in a community which is committed to faithful discipleship including both worship and practical obedience" and notes the contextual advantage of "the extension type of programme" (p. 8). It would be wrong to conclude, however, that Newbigin has joined the TEE "residence seminary" debate on the side of extension training. His concern—and his challenge—is larger and more fundamental. It is a call for renewal of ministry and theological education.

Anil Solanky, then dean of Union Biblical Seminary, Yavatmal, India, sounded the call for renewal even more clearly in another article published in 1978. Solanky had clearly been impressed by the critique of traditional ministry training voiced by TEE advocates, but he was not satisfied with the alternative they offered. He concludes:

> What we need is not just innovations or better methods but a radical change in our concept of education: learning as experience, *versus* gathering content, a body of information. We must treat our students as persons, not as boxes to be filled little by little, with little, logically arranged, packets of information. We must expect them to develop abilities, to grow in the experience of the Lord (II Peter 3:18). (Solanky, p. 133.)

Also in the late 1970s, John Frame of Westminster Theological Seminary, Philadelphia, Pennsylvania, circulated a paper titled, "Proposals for a New North American Model," which was published only in 1984. Frame's dissatisfaction with current approaches to ministry training led him to advocate steps which are truly radical. "I propose first that we dump the academic model once and for all—degrees, accreditation, tenure, the works," he wrote. Frame then outlined an alternative model.

> A church or denomination establishes a kind of "Christian community," where teachers, ministerial candidates, and their families live together, eat together, work together...The Community is not a monastic escape from the world. Rather, it is mobilized for the purpose of establishing and nurturing its members and thrusts them out in the work of planting other churches. Each teacher, student, wife, and child is to be deeply involved in the work of developing churches, through visitation, neighborhood Bible studies, public meetings, street preaching, and then (as churches are established) through Sunday school teaching, preaching, church youth work, church administration, etc. (Frame, pp. 379-380.)

My point is not to argue the appropriateness of Frame's proposals (although they merit sober and biblical review). Rather Frame's article is cited as an example of the rising call for radical reconsideration of ministry and ministry training.

Australian educator Brian Hill's article, "Theological Education: Is It Out of Practice?" also existed for some time before it was published. It is not evident that Hill had interacted with the agencies of renewal reviewed here, but he specifically mentions the engagement of the "laity" in ministry, the Hebraic integration of knowledge and obedience, preference for a master-disciple model of learning, and the teaching that elders should be mature. Drawing on his professional training as an educational philosopher, Hill then identifies "educational strategies" implied by Biblical commitments. He closes his article with an "apocryphal amplification" of verses from Romans 12:

> I urge you brothers (and sisters) in view of God's mercy, to offer your (total personalities) as living sacrifices, holy and pleasing to God.... Do not conform any longer to the pattern of this world (with its Greek and medieval hang-overs) but be transformed by the renewing of your (theological education).... Just as each of us has one body with many members, and these members do not all have the same function, so in Christ we who are many form one body, and each member belongs to all the others (not excluding the full-time clergyman). We have different gifts according to the grace given to us. (Your gift, dear colleague, is to draw out the gifts of others. Do not let your calling become an occasion for stifling the gifts of your people, or for preaching at a level which does not intersect with their life-concerns, or for enjoying a sanctified ego-trip). Be devoted to one another in (filial) love. Honour (your parishioners) above (yourself). (It is just possible that by these means you will be saved from theological hyper-ventilation). (Hill, pp. 181-182.)

In September, 1981, Lois McKinney addressed an evangelical mission executives retreat on the topic, "Why Renewal is Needed in Theological Education." At the time, McKinney served as executive director of CAMEO and was heavily invested in promoting theological education by extension. Nevertheless, a candid review of theological education led her to conclude:

In spite of many successes, and in spite of many encouraging events and trends, both extension and residence programs around the world are badly in need of renewal. The renewal of theological education will come about only as we focus our efforts upon the church, and make its ministry central. Education for ministry will help us to sharpen our goals, to develop appropriate curricula, to individualize instruction, to plan holistically, and to nationalize and contextualize our programs. (McKinney, p. 91).

By far the most penetrating critique of theological education structures, and the most challenging call for renewal of ministry training to be heard in recent years, has come from the pen of Edward Farley. A professor of theology at Vanderbilt University, Farley had devoted considerable attention to the background of the present crisis in theological education. His analysis has led him to disturbing conclusions. Indeed, a complete literature addressing his work has developed, and any current work on renewal of theological education is compelled to interact with his thought. Farley states his conclusions clearly:

I am persuaded that reform attempts will continue to be merely cosmetic until they address the fundamental structure and pattern of studies inherited from the past and submit to criticism the presuppositions which undergird that pattern. I am also persuaded that such a reform, guided by the recovery of theologia, is correlative with a reform of the institutionality of clergy education. This is because the three year course of study occurring on the basis of a typical B.A. degree is drastically insufficient as an education in theological understanding for those who will later be responsible for facilitating it in others. (Farley:1983, p xii.)

Farley's concept of *theologia* is central to his analysis. Simply stated, *theologia* is the knowledge of God—obtained in faith, nurtured by reflection, and evidenced in holistic life. At one time, clergy education was the study of *theologia*—study of the Scriptures (the authoritative deposit of revealed truth) *for the purpose of cultivating theologia* (Farley:1981, p. 96).

Farley charts the fragmentation of "clergy education" through two stages. The unity and integration of ministry training began to unravel in the eighteenth century. Rationalistic challenges to authority stemming from the Enlightenment combined with pursuit of "theological encyclopedia" to de-couple the study of theology from *theologia*. As a result, theological sciences may be (and are) pursued apart from a context of faith. Farley accepts that faith may accompany the study of theological disciplines but notes it is not necessary. This decoupling effect was universalized by acceptance of the fourfold pattern—Bible, church history, dogmatics, and practical theology—for theological education.

Farley dates the current period in clergy education from the 1940s. At that time seminaries became concerned that the education they offered was not preparing graduates for the tasks assigned by their congregations. This resulted in curriculum changes which Farley identifies as "the functionalist form of the clerical paradigm." Although intended to close the divide between seminary and church, the effect was to widen it. Explication of this effect leads to an important recognition for renewal of theological education.

> The education of a leadership for a redemptive community cannot be *defined* by reference to the public tasks and acts by which the community endures (a formal approach), but rather by the requirements set by the nature of that community as redemptive. Defining ministry by its community tasks ignores the community's own redemptive nature, its received tradition, its truth convictions. The very thing that makes theological education important to and related to the church and to the church's leadership, which calls for the various public tasks and sets criteria for their exercise, is absent. Accordingly, the more the external tasks themselves are focused on as the one and only *telos* of theological education, the less the minister becomes qualified to carry them out. This is why the functionalist form of the clerical paradigm promotes and worsens the problem with which it is concerned. (Farley:1983, pp. 127-128.)

Farley's analysis is disturbing, but the implications are clear. Theological education has wandered far from its original mission and is in desperate need of renewal. Furthermore, much of the energy invested in recent efforts toward renewal has been misdirected. The path to renewal of theological education does not lie in more detailed analysis of the tasks of a pastor or more careful preparation for clerical roles. Renewal—true renewal—must begin with a more biblical understanding of the church and leadership in the church.

After his insightful analysis, Farley's proposals for renewal are disappointing, to say the least. One comment captures the essence of Farley's contribution and the current status of renewal in theological education: "In our judgment, [Farley] is unsurpassed as a diagnostician. What remains to be developed is a compelling prescription to cure the disease" (Stackhouse, p. 135).

Summary

Powerful forces have been—and are—at work to press the need for renewal of theological education. Heavily funded projects of the Association of Theological Schools in the United States and Canada have focused on the status of North American ministry training and the need for renewal. The international missionary movement, and specifically the Theological Education Fund, has addressed the inadequacy of western programs for equipping leaders for the Church in the Two-Thirds World. Theological education by extension (TEE) has brought home the fact that alternative models of training exist and has made seminary faculty aware of educational issues not previously discussed. And individual voices, particularly Edward Farley's, have called attention to the need for renewal of theological education.

All this provides the context for renewal efforts by the International Council of Accrediting Agencies for Evangelical Theological Education (ICAA). That story, however, belongs to the following chapter.

CHAPTER 2

The ICAA Manifesto:
Its History And Values

The project known as the International Council of Accrediting Agencies for Evangelical Theological Education (ICAA) is relatively recent, but commitment within the World Evangelical Fellowship (WEF) to renewal of theological education antedates the founding of ICAA by many years.

Early Concern within WEF
For Renewal of Theological Education

Although "commissions" have been part of the WEF structure from its founding in 1951, Howard records that the commission structure did not function prior to 1969 (Howard, p. 157). At the 1968 meeting of the WEF General Council, Rev. Bruce Nicholls, a missionary from New Zealand who served on the faculty of Union Biblical Seminary, Yeotmal, India, presented a thoughtful paper identifying theological trends and problems facing the church. At the same meeting a Theological Commission was created and Nicholls was named Theological Coordinator.

Members were not appointed to the Theological Commission until 1974, but Nicholls single-handedly launched a vigorous program of assistance to evangelical theological schools, known as the Theological Assistance Program of WEF (TAP). Evangelical schools had largely been denied access to programs of the Theological Education Fund, then in its Second Mandate period, and TAP seemed an appropriate vehicle for delivering the assistance so sorely needed. Projects proposed and initiated by Nicholls included:

> ...theological publications, consultations on theological problems, leadership training, curriculum development for training schools, biblical library funds for schools, accreditation

for theological colleges, evangelical research centres, programming for Theological Education by Extension, and regional theological societies. (Howard, pp. 158-159.)

Nicholls' role in WEF and his leadership in TAP made him an obvious choice when organizers of the 1974 International Congress On World Evangelization, Lausanne, Switzerland, sought a speaker to address the topic, "Theological Education and Evangelization." In the paper presented, Nicholls articulated a six-point strategy in theological education. A list of Nicholls' points is instructive:

1. Objectives in theological education
2. The integration of academic, spiritual, and practical in theological education
3. Restructuring the curriculum design
4. New patterns of theological training
5. Articulation of the theology of evangelization
6. Cooperation through a network of relationships (Nicholls:1975.)

Although the topic of renewal of theological education *per se* had not been broached to this point within the WEF, Nicholls raised the issues of renewal. Under his fourth point, furthermore, he made specific mention of the need for renewal.

We must continue to emphasize the importance of *residential training*. The traditional pattern of three-four years full-time training for the evangelistic, parish, and mission ministries of the Church needs constant renewal and is crucial to the Church as an institution. (Nicholls:1975, p. 641.)

He proceeded, then, to note the contribution of "vacational and one-year residential courses for laymen," "short refresher courses for ministers and missionaries," and "Theological Education by Extension."
The report of the Lausanne Theological Education and Evangelization Strategy Group incorporated many of Nicholls' points but spoke even more directly of the need for renewal.

Theological training programs intended to equip pastoral and evangelistic ministry in many cases are outmoded and antiquated. Any advance in this crucial area must begin with a reconsideration of the basic objectives of theological education. Irrespective of the level sought, attention must be given to the integrated development of the student's total person in his *being, knowing,* and *doing,* to the end that the man of God be equipped:

1. To lead others to commitment to Jesus Christ as Savior and Lord,
2. To sustain in commitment those who have believed,
3. To mobilize the church to effective evangelistic activity.
   (Douglas, p. 646.)

Both the suggestion that incumbent training programs are "outmoded and antiquated," and the call for "reconsideration of the basic objectives of theological education" echo renewal concerns. Nevertheless, the Strategy Group failed to go beyond Nicholls' program for strengthening (vs. renewing) theological education structures.

Immediately following the meetings in Lausanne, the WEF Sixth General Assembly was convened at Chateau d'Oex, Switzerland. It was at this time that eleven theological educators from nine nations were appointed to the Theological Commission. Howard reports:

Dr. John Stott addressed the assembly on the question of regional theological associations, suggesting that a fellowship of theologians should be encouraged nationally and regionally, and that theological education should be critically reconsidered. (Howard, p. 161.)

Nicholls left Chateau d'Oex to draft an editorial for *Theological News,* titled "Means of Renewal." The editorial builds on the report of the Lausanne "Theological Education and Evangelization Strategy Group," employing the opening sentence cited above. What follows is not the critical reconsideration of theological education Stott called for, however, but affirmation of "the distinct advantage" of "the residential pattern" and a challenge to establish "a chain of [theological research] centres encircling the globe" (Nicholls:1974). Sadly, *Theological News* did not return to the topic of renewal of theological education until 1982—and then in an article run under the masthead of *Theological Education Today.*

Nicholls' sensitivity to the environmental factors described in the previous chapter (especially the TEF) led him to adopt the rhetoric of renewal, even though the need *per se* had yet to crystallize in his thinking. In September 1975 the WEF Theological Commission met in London, with a report subsequently published under the title *Defending and Confirming the Gospel*. The concerns of the meeting were largely theological, but Nicholls included a section on "Strategies and Structures" which opened with the following statement:

> The emerging role of the Theological Commission of WEF includes:
>
> 1. Maintaining a supporting ministry to all evangelical theological commissions, societies, and associations at regional and national levels....
> 2. Offering a service ministry in specialized areas....
> 3. A catalystic [sic] ministry for more creative theological reflection and renewal in theology and in theological education and in bridging the gap between the layman, the pastor and the theological educator. (Nicholls:1976, p. 16.)

In Nicholls' presentation, a strategy for this catalytic ministry is mentioned only in a section headed, "Stimulating Research and Sponsoring Publications." One of five "priority areas for research" identified by Nicholls is, "research into theological educational methodology in the context of changing educational structures and methods, curriculum design and evaluation" (Nicholls: 1976, p. 26). Identification of research priorities leads to two recommendations: to strengthen research programs and centers where they exist and to encourage regional seminars on priority issues.

The larger emphasis of the 1975 meeting was a focus on accreditation as the principal strategy for "strengthening theological education on six continents." An accreditation association for North American Bible colleges had existed since 1947, but in April 1977 Asia Theological Association (ATA) became the first regional agency in the Two-Thirds World to adopt an accrediting scheme for evangelical schools (*Theological News*:1977a). The Accrediting Council for Theological Education in Africa (ACTEA) approved an accreditation program in August of the same year (*Theological News*:1977b). Two years later, theological educators in Europe and the Caribbean adopted accrediting schemes for their regions (*Theological News*:1979a,b). This set the stage in 1980 for a meeting in Hoddesdon, UK, which resulted in the founding of the International Council of Accrediting Agencies for Evangelical Theological Education (ICAA).

The Renewal Theme within ICAA: 1980-1987

Responsibility for planning the Hoddesdon consultation was delegated to Paul Bowers, an American missionary to Nigeria who had been active in ACTEA from its inception. In the keynote address, Nicholls assessed the task of theological educators in the 1980s, then offered five proposals for "restructuring" theological education:

> Refining educational objectives
> Diversifying educational programmes
> Reinforcing education by extension
> Expanding educational methodologies
> Promoting educational accreditation
> (Nicholls:1982a, pp. 16-23.)

The first four proposals clearly reflect renewal concerns. Nicholls views TEE as a complement to residential school programs, however, apparently unaware of TEE's significance as a step toward renewal of theological education. In view of the consultation agenda, Nicholls gave fullest treatment to his fifth proposal. Ro's paper, presented the next evening, followed with ten proposals for accreditation programs and services.

The other two papers presented at Hoddesdon, by McKinney and Chow, dealt more directly with renewal themes. McKinney urged the founders of ICAA to attend to the broad spectrum of training needs in the Church, to employ an outcomes assessment approach to program evaluation, and to encourage a cultural response to Biblical imperatives. Chow argued that integration of communal life, academic study, and field training can lead to significant improvement (renewal) of traditional seminary programs. Both of these papers were scheduled for the closing afternoon, however, so they had little bearing on the direction of the consultation or the decisions of delegates.

At Hoddesdon, nevertheless, renewal of theological education was placed on the agenda of ICAA. In 1981, when the second ICAA consultation was convened in Chongoni, Malawi, the announced theme was "The Renewal of Evangelical Theological Education." Tokunboh Adeyemo, a Nigerian who served as general secretary of the Association of Evangelicals of Africa and Madagascar, provided a keynote address which plunged straight to the heart of the matter.

What is renewal and how does it come about? to renew is to restore to an original state, to make as good as new, to revive, to regenerate...In our theological education process renewal may demand flexibility as opposed to rigidity, freedom of the Spirit as opposed to legalism, and originality of symbolism and thought-forms as opposed to traditionalism. Of necessity, our pedagogy will shift emphasis from formal to informal, from 'communication to' to 'communication with,' from clandestine individualism to community, from obligation to commitment, and from mere display of talents to discovering, developing, and deploying the charismata. (Adeyemo, pp. 11-12.)

As the consultation proceeded, Nicholls called for new attention to spiritual formation of ministerial trainees, Tiènou focused the need for contextualization of training, and Plueddemann drew attention to the neglected responsibility to view ministry training in a Biblical and theological perspective. None of the theological educators came to grips with the core issues of renewal, however, as did Adeyemo, the churchman.

It was Bowers' paper, titled "Accreditation as a Catalyst for Renewal in Theological Education," which moved the ICAA to action. The Council accepted his proposal to draw up "a manifesto on the renewal of evangelical theological education" and assigned to him the responsibility for drafting the document. We will return shortly to examine Bowers' fulfillment of this task.

As early as 1975, it was suggested that accreditation services should be extended to TEE programs (Nicholls:1976, p. 23). Although the ICAA Council met annually for business, no consultation was held in 1982 or 1983. When a consultation was convened at Skouriotissa, Cyprus, in 1984, the theme was TEE. According to the pattern already established, TEE was dealt with as an alternative model of training, with little notice taken of its significance for theological education and its renewal.

This convenient perception was jarred, however, by Ferris' paper on "The Future of Theological Education." He had been invited to present a paper on the future of TEE, but Ferris broadened his topic to include the significance of TEE for theological education as a field. He opened his paper with mention of a biological process of renewal in which "structures which become too cumbersome or conflict with each other" are "degraded, pruned back to their more essential roots." Ferris commented:

I would submit that the issues with which we wrestle are much larger than the significance of theological education by extension. Ten years from now, fifty years from now, TEE may or may not survive as an approach to ministry formation. My greater concern is for the 'degrading' process present in TEE. If that process is thwarted, it is the future significance of theological education itself which is in jeopardy. (Ferris:1986, p. 43.)

Three years elapsed before another ICAA consultation was convened. Robert Youngblood, then Executive Secretary of ICAA, recognized that concern for excellence and renewal in theological education lay at the center of ICAA's mission. In June 1987 a consultation in Unterweissach, West Germany, was planned around those themes. Four of the five papers which came out of the consultation addressed the concern for renewal.

Speaking to "The Challenge of Excellence," James Plueddemann of Wheaton College (USA) argued that the key to renewal is "intentional and regular efforts to compel interaction between the world of ideas and the world of the senses, between absolutes and specifics, between theory and practice" (1989, p. 9). This, Plueddemann insisted, "requires a revolutionary paradigm shift" in the design and methodology of theological education. He urges accrediting agencies to take the lead in promoting this paradigm shift and, thus, renewal of theological education.

Terry Hulbert, of Columbia Bible College and Seminary (USA), spoke to "The Challenge in Renewal." Hulbert argued that renewal of theological education is urgently needed, lamented that churches are weak, observed that theological schools contribute little to the task of world evangelism, and warned that faith is being challenged. He reminded the accreditors that their agencies "have the credibility and authority to make good things happen." He insisted that accrediting agencies are more than caretakers of academic mores. They are really visionaries peering over the horizon. (Hulbert:1989, p. 31.)

Ken Gnanakan, of ACTS Institute, Bangalore, India, stressed the "refreshing" work of God the Holy Spirit in a paper on "Accreditation and Renewal." Gnanakan noted that "God's renewal of his work is seen primarily when there is an urge to return to basics" (Gnanakan:1989, p. 49). This led him to reflect on theological education's role in cultivating in learners a longing to know God, a focus on ministry to people, a life shaped by biblical values, and relevant expression of faith in cultural context. Along the way Gnanakan pressed the critical need for accrediting agencies to be active promoters of these emphases in theological education.

The final paper to address renewal at Unterweissach was presented by Robert Ferris. He was scheduled to report on an ICAA/Asia Theological Association project to develop an accreditation scheme for TEE. He concluded his presentation, however, with a challenge for ICAA regional agencies to promote renewal of theological education through their accreditation programs. Noting that the ICAA "Manifesto" affirms a "longing and prayer for the renewal of evangelical theological education today," Ferris pressed the practical implications of this commitment.

> Do we long and pray for renewal? We must go further. Let us ask how our commitment to renewal of theological education bears on our accreditation structures. Let us recognize the conservationist bent of accreditation which flows against the movement toward renewal. Let us acknowledge that accreditation structures which are oriented to the artifacts and procedures of schooling are a threat not only to renewal in TEE, but to renewal in campus theological training as well. (Ferris:1989, p. 78.)

It is unfortunate that the Unterweissach consultation was overshadowed by organizational difficulties within ICAA which precluded any definitive commitment or action in response to the papers on renewal.

In the first seven years of ICAA's existence, therefore, renewal of theological education was repeatedly raised and examined. No specific action was taken, however, except for issuing the "Manifesto on the Renewal of Evangelical Theological Education." For that reason it is important to take a closer look at the development, content, and use of the Manifesto.

Development of the ICAA Manifesto

As noted above, the proposal to issue a manifesto on renewal of evangelical theological education was first advanced by Bowers in his paper presented in Malawi in September 1981. Bowers was concerned that "traditionalists" and "radicalists" were expending effort in fruitless debate, while large and important areas of consensus between them were passing unattended. His intention was to set forth a clear and positive statement of basic renewal values. The Council immediately adopted Bowers' proposal and assigned him to prepare a draft for discussion.

Bowers had included in his paper seven points as "a brief sampling ... of the agenda which has achieved broad consensus among evangelical theological educators internationally" (Bowers:1982a, p. 34). Through discussion with colleagues and reflection on the papers presented at Hoddesdon and Malawi, Bowers expanded this list to eighteen. In April 1982 he cast these into a "Very Preliminary Draft" which he distributed to about two dozen theological educators on all continents. A number of these individuals responded to offer comment and advice on the document.

In light of these responses, Bowers recast the Manifesto into a "Preliminary Draft in Progress" which was discussed by the ICAA Council at its September 1982 meeting in Seoul, Korea. The Council agreed that the document deserved careful study and that comments for further adjustments should be forwarded to Bowers in Nairobi. Bowers reports that comments were received, resulting in a further editing of the draft Manifesto. This edited draft was adopted by the ICAA Council at its meetings held in Wheaton, Illinois, in July 1983.

Table 1 compares the points included in the various drafts. In its adopted form the Manifesto combines contrition for past sins with resolve to more conscientiously strive toward the values affirmed.

The Manifesto was published in *Evangelical Review of Theology* and in the Theological Education Today section of *Theological News*. It is ironic that no official printing of the Manifesto has been prepared due to an editorial dispute over the wording of the introductory paragraphs. That was finally resolved with adoption, in June 1989, of a lengthy introduction describing the purpose and process of the Manifesto's preparation. Perhaps at last the Manifesto will receive broader distribution.

The need for renewal of evangelical theological education was evident—and to some extent, recognized—from the inception of WEF's active attention to ministry training issues. Programs of the Theological Assistance Program and, subsequently, the International Council of Accrediting Agencies have focused on buttressing incumbent training structures, however, rather than seriously promoting renewal.

TABLE 2.1

Evolution Of The ICAA Manifesto

Bowers' Paper September 1981	Preliminary Draft April 1982	Draft in Progress September 1982	Adopted Draft July 1983
Curricular Contextualization	Curricular Contextualization	Contextualization	Contextualization
Outcomes Measurement	Outcomes Measurement	Churchward Orientation	Churchward Orientation
Ministerial Styles	Churchward Orientation	Strategic Flexibility	Strategic Flexibility
Integrated Program	Servant Moulding	Theological Grounding	Theological Grounding
Field Learning	Community Life	Continuous Assessment	Continuous Assessment
Spiritual Formation	Integrated Programming	Servant Molding [sic]	Community Life
Churchward Orientation	Spiritual Formation	Community Life	Integrated Programme
	Theological Focusing	Integrated Programme	Servant Moulding
	Practical Equipping	Equipping For Growth	Instructional Variety
	Service by Objective	A Christian Mind	A Christian Mind
	Outcomes Measurement	Cooperation	Equipping For Growth
	Voluntary Accountability		Cooperation
	Pursuit of Excellence		
	Continuous Review		
	Theological Grounding		
	Methodological Breadth		
	Model Breadth		
	Cooperative Initiatives		

Summary

The issue of renewal has surfaced repeatedly in the short history of the WEF Theological Commission and the ICAA, constantly being reintroduced by the environmental forces described in the previous chapter. Enthusiasm for renewal is difficult to find within the WEF Theological Commission and the ICAA, however. The result is an interesting—and often discouraging—interplay between an issue which refuses to be ignored and an association which lacks commitment to the agenda at hand.

It is possible, of course, that renewal of theological education is a pseudo-issue which deserves to be treated with benign neglect. Perhaps renewal of theological education is simply a topic for scholarly discussion among those who wish to be identified as *avant garde*. Maybe ICAA's disinterest in renewal reflects a similar apathy within the field of theological education. To test the reality of the need for renewal we must inquire into the concerns and commitment of theological educators. The next chapter reports on a survey which took up this task.

CHAPTER 3

The Place Of Renewal in Institutional Commitments[5]

The fundamental presupposition of the "Manifesto" is the perception that today there is a wide agreement among evangelical theological educators on the need for renewal in theological education and on an agenda for such renewal. (ICAA:1984, p. 136.)

Thus the prologue to the ICAA "Manifesto on the Renewal of Evangelical Theological Education" states its underlying assumption, but are these perceptions accurate? Is there "wide agreement" among evangelicals on the need for renewal of theological education? Is the agenda articulated in the ICAA Manifesto an accurate reflection of the values, aspirations, and commitments held by evangelical theological educators today?

To test these questions, and to ascertain the Manifesto's impact as a stimulus to renewal, a research strategy was developed calling for two surveys. The first polled the directors of ICAA member agencies. The instrument employed inquired regarding the director's awareness of the ICAA Manifesto, level of commitment to the renewal values articulated in the Manifesto, and past, present, or anticipated use of the Manifesto as a stimulus toward renewal.[6] The survey instrument was sent to the directors of all six ICAA member agencies[7] with 100% rate of response.

A second survey addressed the 242 institutions worldwide which are accredited by these agencies.[8] This was viewed as a select sample of evangelical theological education institutions, arguably many of the world's best. Because of their close identification with ICAA member agencies, furthermore, theological educators in these institutions are favorably positioned to know of the Manifesto and to benefit from efforts by accreditation agencies to promote renewal of theological education.

The first challenge in developing an appropriate instrument arose from the length (2500 words) of the Manifesto. A condensed version was prepared by excerpting lead sentences from each of the Manifesto's twelve points. This condensation was edited to produce a list of "Twelve Values for Renewal," with definitions (see Table 3.1). Although the resulting list does not echo the terminology of the Manifesto at every point, it seeks to give focused expression to the renewal values articulated in the larger document.

A survey instrument was developed to determine theological educators' level of commitment to renewal of theological education, commitment to the "renewal values" derived from the Manifesto, and awareness of ICAA and the Manifesto. This instrument was distributed to the 242 schools worldwide accredited by ICAA member agencies. Table 3.2 reflects the distribution of the survey instrument and the rate of response.

Table 3.1

Twelve Values for Renewal of Evangelical Theological Education

A. **Cultural Appropriateness**—Training is referenced to the traditions, conditions, and needs in the local society, and is responsive to shifts in social norms and values.

B. **Attentiveness to the Church**—Basic orientation is toward the constituent church, rather than academia. Input from churchmen is actively sought and is accorded highest priority in development, delivery, and assessment of training programs.

C. **Flexible Strategizing**—Educators are aware of the broad spectrum of training needs which may exist in the constituent church, sensitive to needs which do exist, and creative in responding to needs with appropriate training programs.

D. **Theological Grounding**—The task and guiding values of theological education are derived from and rooted in a Biblical theology of creation, redemption, church, and ministry.

E. **Outcomes Assessment**—The value of education is determined by examining alumni performance in ministry (vs. resources and instructional procedures in the training institution).

F.   **Spiritual Formation**—A community life is cultivated which promotes and facilitates growth in grace.

G.   **Holistic Curricularizing**—Academic, practical, and spiritual training is integrated into a unified program of professional development.

H.   **Service Orientation**—Emphasis is placed on leadership as servanthood; elitist attitudes are consciously renounced.

I.   **Creativity in Teaching**—Teaching methods are selected reflectively or developed creatively to correlate with instructional goals.

J.   **A Christian Worldview**—Training seeks to cultivate a mindset in which the Bible is the standard for measuring every area of life and thought.

K.   **A Developmental Focus**—Faculty-student interactions are deliberately designed to encourage and facilitate self-directed learning; methods cultivating dependencies are resolutely resisted.

L.   **A Cooperative Spirit**—Institutional leadership is committed to open communication and collaboration among evangelical theological education institutions.

Table 3.2

Schools Survey Distribution and Responses

Agency

American Association of Bible Colleges	87	52	60%
Accrediting Council for Theological Education in Africa	18	12	67%
Asia Theological Association	47	38	81%
Caribbean Evangelical Theological Association	20	9	45%
European Evangelical Accrediting Association	22	10	45%
South Pacific Association of Bible Colleges	14	14	100%
Fellowship of Evangelical Seminary Presidents	34	26	76%
TOTALS	242	161	67%

Findings Which Raise Questions

Analysis of survey responses presents a bad news/good news story. The ICAA member agencies survey findings would qualify, on the whole, as bad news. All six agencies agreed that renewal is needed in theological education (I consider that good news), but four of six agency leaders described themselves as only "somewhat familiar" or "slightly familiar" with the ICAA Manifesto.[9]

Furthermore, three of six agencies report they have made no use of the Manifesto, have not found the Manifesto a significant stimulus toward renewal, and have no plans to use it in the future. These findings raise questions which beg for clarification.

Agency leaders were also asked to rate the frequency with which renewal values (as stated in the Manifesto) are evidenced among the schools of their region. On a seven-point opinion scale (1 = No Schools, 4 is midpoint, and 7 = All Schools), respondents tended toward a mid-range assessment of renewal values in affiliated institutions. (Mean across all twelve renewal values was 4.12.[10])

When asked to rate the priority they assign to promoting renewal values within their region, on the other hand, agency leaders responded somewhat more positively (mean across twelve values was 5.22, with 1 = Unimportant and 7 = Highest Priority). Mean scores have little meaning when the number of subjects is only six, however; closer examination shows that five of the twelve items yielded a bimodal response pattern.[11] This seems to indicate differences in values among ICAA member agencies which invite more careful exploration.

One would expect that these two items would correlate negatively—that is, when a renewal value is relatively common the priority attached to its promotion would be minimal, while values rarely demonstrated would merit higher priority in promotion. The items did correlate negatively for three agencies, but for the other three, surprisingly, correlation was very low.[12] This raises questions regarding the way some accrediting agencies establish their educational services agenda and presents yet another topic for further study.

Unfortunately, the bad news is not limited to findings of the ICAA members survey. Survey responses received from 161 accredited institutions reveal that ICAA is a well-kept secret. As indicated in Table 3.3, fewer than one respondent in four (only 23.8%) reported being "very aware" of ICAA.

Table 3.3

Theological Educators' Awareness of ICAA

REGION RESPONSE	US-SEMS n=26	AABC n=52	ACTEA n=12	ATA n=38	CETA n= 9	EEAA n=10	SPABC n=14	TOTAL n=161	%	Valid %
Not Aware	9	26	0	6	1	0	0	42	26.1%	26.3%
Somewhat Aware	14	21	9	20	4	7	5	80	49.7%	50.0%
Very Aware	3	5	3	11	4	3	9	38	23.6%	23.8%
No Response	0	0	0	1	0	0	0	1	.6%	—

Even more discouraging, however, is theological educators' level of familiarity with the Manifesto as reported in Table 3.4. Over 85% of the heads of accredited theological institutions indicated they are not familiar with the basic contents of the Manifesto (72.4%) or they are not sure of its contents (12.8%)! Since ICAA adopted the Manifesto at its 1983 meetings, one wonders why it has received so little exposure over the past six years. The agencies affirm their commitment to renewal in the strongest terms, yet the Manifesto is inadequately promoted (even among affiliated institutions), rarely used, and little known. Are the issues identified in the Manifesto not central to renewal after all? Does the length and style of the text inhibit its usefulness? Or has preoccupation with maintenance of agencies and institutions precluded attention to issues which, in fact, lie close to ICAA's calling and mission? One senses these questions, raised by the survey findings, ought not be passed over quickly.

Table 3.4

Theological Educators' Familiarity with the *ICAA Manifesto*

REGION RESPONSE	US-SEMS n=26	AABC n=52	ACTEA n=12	ATA n=38	CETA n= 9	EEAA n=10	SPABC n=14	TOTAL n=161	%	Valid %
Not Familiar	21	44	7	22	6	6	7	113	70.2%	72.4%
Not Sure	1	3	1	9	1	3	2	20	12.4%	12.8%
Familiar	4	3	3	6	2	1	4	23	14.3%	14.7%
No Response	0	2	1	1	0	0	1	5	3.1%	----

Renewal Is a Felt Need Among ICAA Related Schools

Enough of the bad news; there is plenty of good news as well. The survey on "Renewal of Evangelical Theological Education" clearly touched a sensitive nerve with many school leaders. The 67% rate of return on the instrument must be considered gratifying by common standards of postal survey research. Furthermore, although the questionnaire instrument was nine pages long, 94% of the respondents were chief executive officers (i.e., president, principal, or dean) of their institution. This is not a questionnaire which was assigned to a junior instructor or secretary to complete. Beyond that, fully 55% of respondents requested a report of the findings of the study *despite the fact that there was no check-off space on the instrument to accommodate that request.* In this light, it seems conservative to conclude that the leaders of evangelical Bible and theological schools are interested in renewal.

When institutional respondents were asked if renewal of theological education is needed, they answered with a resounding affirmative.[13] The instrument next asked if present approaches to ministry training are "serving us well," or if "major change is needed." Respondents were less emphatic, but clearly affirmed that major change is needed.[14]

Strong affirmation of a need for renewal and change leads one to wonder what theological educators mean by "renewal of theological education"—what is it they intend to affirm? When asked in an open ended item "What changes are needed to renew theological education?," responses varied widely. Content analysis yielded eight distinct categories representing 4% or more of the total response, as reported in Table 3.5. No consensus was observed in responses to this item.

Table 3.5

Factors Proposed as Contributing to Renewal
n = 161

FACTOR	f.	%	VALID %
Refocus on Serving the Church	26	16.1%	17.9%
Refocus on Addressing Cultural Issues	22	13.7%	15.2%
Stronger Integration of Theology and Practice	22	13.7%	15.2%
Stronger Emphasis on Bible and Theology	20	12.4%	13.8%
Stronger Emphasis on Ministry Skills	15	9.3%	10.3%
Stronger Emphasis on Spiritual Formation	10	6.2%	6.9%
Refocus on Evangelism and Missions	9	5.6%	6.2%
Stronger Emphasis on Scholarship	7	4.3%	4.8%
Other (Fewer than 4% per category)	14	8.7%	9.7%
No Response	16	9.9%	0.0%
Total	161	100.0%	100.0%

It would appear that any confusion is more a matter of expressing renewal values, however, than of recognizing them. When presented with the twelve renewal values derived from the Manifesto, respondents emphatically owned these values (Table 3.6). It is not encouraging to realize that the commitment of some regional agencies to renewal ideals lags behind that of schools they accredit.[15] Nevertheless, these findings appear to offer strong support for the presupposition stated in the Manifesto prologue.

Table 3.6

Affirmation of Renewal Values by Theological Educators
(Scale: 1=Unimportant; 7=Extremely Important)

RENEWAL VALUE	REGION	US-SEMS n=26	AABC n=52	ACTEA n=12	ATA n=38	CETA n= 9	EEAA n=10	SPABC n=14	TOTAL n=161
Cultural	μ	5.500	5.692	6.250	6.289	5.667	5.400	6.214	5.870
Appropriateness	σ	1.105	1.130	.622	.984	.866	1.075	.699	1.050
Attentiveness	μ	6.115	6.000	6.250	6.027	6.000	5.700	6.071	6.031
To the Church	σ	.816	1.188	.754	1.424	.707	1.059	.917	1.107
Flexible	μ	5.920	6.115	6.167	5.947	6.000	5.500	6.214	6.013
Strategizing	σ	.862	.943	.718	1.089	.866	.850	.802	.932
Theological	μ	6.923	6.808	6.909	6.816	6.556	6.667	6.714	6.805
Grounding	σ	.272	.445	.302	.563	.882	.500	.825	.521
Outcomes	μ	6.077	6.180	6.167	6.263	5.778	5.889	5.571	6.089
Assessment	σ	.845	.774	.835	1.245	1.093	.601	1.697	1.037
Spiritual	μ	6.692	6.490	6.667	6.684	6.778	6.400	6.786	6.619
Formation	σ	.549	.674	.492	.662	.667	.516	.426	.613
Holistic	μ	6.500	6.353	6.583	6.579	6.444	6.300	6.714	6.481
Curricularizing	σ	.648	.744	.669	.683	.882	.949	.469	.709
Service	μ	6.000	6.423	6.500	6.500	6.444	6.400	6.571	6.394
Orientation	σ	1.190	.723	.522	.762	.726	.699	.514	.802
Creative	μ	6.160	6.231	6.250	5.816	5.667	5.800	6.286	6.069
Teaching	σ	.987	.703	.754	1.111	1.118	.632	.726	.898
Christian	μ	6.769	6.712	6.667	6.514	6.000	6.400	6.929	6.631
Worldview	σ	.514	.498	.492	.961	1.323	.699	.267	.715
Developmental	μ	5.615	5.788	5.917	6.135	5.778	5.889	5.643	5.843
Focus	σ	1.098	.723	.793	.918	1.302	.601	1.598	.971
Cooperative	μ	6.000	5.569	6.000	6.316	5.667	5.600	6.07	5.900
Spirit	σ	.748	1.082	.953	.620	1.414	1.075	.917	.966

Having established that renewal values are important to theological educators, the instrument next asked if those values were demonstrated in their schools. Although respondents obviously wanted to provide a positive report, Table 3.7 shows they consistently rated demonstration

lower than the level of importance assigned to renewal values.[16] This
gap between affirmation of renewal values and demonstration of those

Table 3.7

Affirmation and Demonstration of Renewal Values
Mean Responses by Theological Educators
(Scale: 1=Unimportant; 7=Extremely Important)

RENEWAL VALUE	REGION	US-SEMS n=26	AABC n=52	ACTEA n=12	ATA n=38	CETA n=9	EEAA n=10	SPABC n=14	TOTAL n=161
Cultural	Aff	5.500	5.692	6.250	*6.289	*5.667	5.400	*6.214	*5.870
Appro	Dem	4.577	4.904	5.333	4.811	4.556	4.600	4.929	4.825
Attent	Aff	6.115	6.000	*6.250	6.027	6.000	*5.700	6.071	6.031
To Ch	Dem	5.346	5.173	5.000	5.222	5.111	4.600	5.571	5.195
Flex	Aff	*5.920	*6.115	*6.167	5.947	6.000	*5.500	6.214	*6.013
Strat	Dem	4.917	4.846	4.917	5.056	5.000	4.200	5.500	4.936
Theo	Aff	6.923	6.808	6.909	*6.816	6.556	6.667	6.714	6.805
Ground	Dem	6.160	6.000	6.273	5.811	6.000	5.889	6.231	6.013
Outcomes	Aff	<6.077	<6.180	«6.167	*6.263	«5.778	<5.889	<5.571	*6.089
Assess	Dem	4.385	4.840	4.167	5.027	3.778	4.100	3.714	4.551
Spirit	Aff	6.692	6.490	6.667	6.684	*6.778	6.400	6.786	6.619
Form	Dem	5.731	5.627	5.833	5.921	5.333	5.800	5.929	5.750
Holistic	Aff	*6.500	*6.353	*6.583	*6.579	6.444	*6.300	*6.714	*6.481
Curric	Dem	5.385	5.196	5.250	5.447	5.556	4.800	5.286	5.294
Service	Aff	6.000	*6.423	*6.500	*6.500	*6.444	6.400	*6.571	*6.394
Orient	Dem	5.200	5.385	5.167	5.211	5.222	5.500	5.429	5.300
Creative	Aff	<6.160	<6.231	«6.250	*5.816	*5.667	<5.800	<6.286	*6.069
Teach	Dem	4.640	4.712	4.250	4.395	4.333	4.100	4.714	4.531
Christ'n	Aff	6.769	6.712	6.667	6.514	6.000	*6.400	6.929	6.631
Worldv	Dem	5.808	5.712	5.833	5.629	5.286	4.900	6.643	5.731
Develop	Aff	5.615	*5.788	*5.917	*6.135	*5.778	*5.889	5.643	*5.843
Focus	Dem	5.038	4.635	4.583	4.838	4.222	4.444	4.769	4.722
Cooperat	Aff	6.000	5.569	6.000	6.316	5.667	5.600	6.071	5.900
Spirit	Dem	5.400	4.824	5.083	5.500	5.000	5.400	5.714	5.220

Total number of cells = 84
In 84 cells (100%) Level of Affirmation - Level of Demonstration > 0
In 42 cells (50%) Level of Affirmation - Level of Demonstration > 1   (Indicated by *)
In 11 cells (13%) Level of Affirmation - Level of Demonstration > 1.5 (Indicated by <)
In 3 cells (4%) Level of Affirmation - Level of Demonstration > 2   (Indicated by «)

values in ministry training institutions accounts for the observed high level of interest in the study.

Perhaps renewal values are underrepresented in evangelical training programs because they have not received appropriate attention from the faculty and administrators. To check this possibility, the instrument asked educators if the faculty of their school has "deliberately worked on developing" each renewal value in their training program within the last five years. Responses reported in Table 3.9 indicate that is not the problem, since respondents affirm that implementation of renewal values has received extensive attention.

When asked if they can identify other schools which demonstrate renewal values to a high degree, however, fewer than half of the theological educators indicated they could do so.[17]

This presents a very interesting picture. Theological educators affirm renewal values but admit that demonstration of those values in their own institutions falls short of their commitment. This disappointing status exists despite deliberate efforts to realize these values. Furthermore, theological educators do not know of other schools that are doing better.

It would appear that a golden opportunity exists for renewal of ministry training. Renewal values are embraced, and educators are eager for change. They only lack models that show them how to implement the values they affirm.

Finally, the cover letter mailed with the survey instrument stated clearly that the values presented were taken from the ICAA Manifesto, and this was repeated in the instrument instructions. The last item on the instrument asked respondents if they would "like to know more about ICAA and its efforts to promote renewal of evangelical theological education." As Table 3.8 reports, fully 92.4% of respondents requested more information. This should come as good news to ICAA and its regional agencies. If accrediting agencies can move definitively to help schools experience renewal of ministry training programs, a

Table 3.8

Theological Educators Requesting Information About ICAA

RESPONSE	REGION US-SEMS	AABC	ACTEA	ATA	CETA	EEAA	SPABC		TOTAL	
	n=26	n=52	n=12	n=38	n=9	n=10	n=14	n=161	%	Valid %
Please Send	25	45	12	34	9	9	12	146	90.7%	92.4%
Not Needed	1	7	0	1	0	1	2	12	7.5%	7.6%
No Response	0	0	0	3	0	0	0	3	1.9%	—

Table 3.9

Deliberate Attempts to Implement Renewal Values

VALUE	AGENCY	US-SEMS n=26	AABC n=52	ACTEA n=12	ATA n=38	CETA n=9	EEAA n=10	SPABC n=14	n=161	TOTAL %	Valid %
Cultural	| Yes	18	41	12	30	7	8	12	128	79.5%	80.5%
Appro	| No	8	11	0	8	1	1	2	31	19.3%	19.5%
	Nul	0	0	0	0	1	1	0	2	1.2%	—
Attent	| Yes	24	44	11	32	9	10	11	141	87.6%	88.7%
To Ch	| No	2	8	1	5	0	0	2	18	11.2%	11.3%
	Nul	0	0	0	1	0	0	1	2	1.2%	—
Flex	| Yes	24	33	12	28	8	8	12	125	77.6%	83.3%
Strat	| No	1	13	0	9	1	1	0	25	15.5%	16.7%
	Nul	0	6	0	1	0	1	2	11	6.8%	—
Theo	| Yes	22	43	10	35	5	7	11	133	82.6%	89.3%
Ground	| No	4	5	0	2	3	0	2	16	9.9%	10.7%
	Nul	0	4	2	1	1	3	1	12	7.5%	—
Outcomes	| Yes	17	38	10	30	2	9	6	112	69.6%	72.3%
Assess	| No	8	11	1	8	6	1	8	43	26.7%	27.7%
	Nul	1	3	1	0	1	0	0	6	3.7%	—
Spirit	| Yes	25	44	12	36	7	10	12	146	90.7%	93.0%
Form	| No	1	7	0	1	2	0	0	11	6.8%	7.0%
	Nul	0	1	0	1	0	0	2	4	2.5%	—
Holistic	| Yes	22	41	11	35	6	8	9	132	82.0%	86.3%
Curric	| No	3	6	1	3	3	2	3	21	13.0%	13.7%
	Nul	1	5	0	0	0	0	2	8	5.0%	—
Service	| Yes	14	32	11	29	5	7	12	110	68.3%	74.8%
Orient	| No	9	16	0	5	3	2	2	37	23.0%	25.2%
	Nul	3	4	1	4	1	1	0	14	8.7%	—
Creative	| Yes	20	43	7	25	5	7	11	118	73.3%	74.7%
Teach	| No	6	8	3	13	4	3	3	40	24.8%	25.3%
	Nul	0	1	2	0	0	0	0	3	1.9%	—
Christ'n	| Yes	17	39	7	29	3	7	9	111	68.9%	75.0%
Worldv	| No	8	10	4	6	5	1	3	37	23.0%	25.0%
	Nul	1	3	1	3	1	2	2	13	8.1%	—
Develop	| Yes	14	23	6	29	5	6	10	93	57.8%	62.0%
Focus	| No	11	25	4	7	4	3	3	57	35.4%	38.0%
	Nul	1	4	2	2	0	1	1	11	6.8%	—
Cooperat	| Yes	20	26	11	34	6	8	12	117	72.7%	76.0%
Spirit	| No	5	22	1	4	3	1	1	37	23.0%	24.0%
	Nul	1	4	0	0	0	1	1	7	4.3%	—

declared objective of the agencies will be realized while meeting a deeply felt need of their principal constituency. Theological accreditors need not drum up enthusiasm or sell an unpopular program; they need only to provide the educational services member institutions long for.

Models of Renewal

It would appear that a major inhibitor of renewal of theological education is a lack of information among evangelical educators regarding innovations in ministry training worldwide. As survey responses were received and reviewed, it was not difficult to identify institutions which have recognized and addressed the need for renewal. In each region some schools have mustered the courage and creativity to experiment with alternative models of ministry training. In no case has renewal touched every aspect of institutional life, but in many cases significant strides have been made in one or more areas.

In order to examine these experiments more closely, the research design provided for visits to several institutions which illustrate how renewal values can be realized. The chapters which follow report observations made during those visits.

CHAPTER 4

Canadian Bible College and Canadian Theological Seminary
Regina, Saskatchewan

Canadian Bible College (CBC) and Canadian Theological Seminary (CTS) are schools of the Christian and Missionary Alliance (C&MA) of Canada, located in Regina, Saskatchewan. Although the schools have separate faculties, curricula, and students, they share a common administration and a common campus. CBC and CTS demonstrate attentiveness to the Church and outcomes assessment.

Evidence of Attentiveness to the Church at CBC/CTS

Institutional structures provide strong ties between CBC/CTS and the C&MA in Canada. The president of the Alliance is an ex-officio member of the schools' Board of Governors, and the superintendents of all five Canadian districts serve as members of the board. Likewise, CBC/CTS faculty are voting members of the Canadian Midwest District of the C&MA and the national General Assembly, held biennially. The president of the schools presents biennial reports to the General Assembly and the five district conferences.

These formal linkages are buttressed and strengthened by a healthy flow of communication and goodwill between the church and the schools. Tangible evidence of that goodwill is seen in the excellent facilities of the institution. The sixteen-acre campus and thirteen buildings, including five residence halls, a modern cafeteria (completed in 1975), and gymnasium/auditorium (also 1975), the seminary building (1979), a spacious library expansion (1980), and a chapel with seating for 1100 (1982) are all debt free, attesting to the generous support the schools enjoy from Alliance congregations across Canada.

Internship Program with Instruction by Pastors

The institution's commitment to listen to the church is seen in its internship program. During the early 1970s, Alliance pastors and district superintendents became convinced that ministry preparation could be enhanced by a period of field training. As a result of a brainstorming session attended by six leading pastors, a proposal for a pilot internship program was presented to the institution in 1972. CBC now requires at least a three-month internship for all professional degree programs (i.e., B.Th., B.R.E., and B.S.M.), and CTS specifies the same requirement for all seminary students.

The internship program is administered by the institution's Director of Ministry Placement, but instruction is given by Alliance pastors. The program has been so well received by Alliance congregations that the administrator currently selects churches annually to be invited into the program and is forced to turn down many that request interns. The value of the internship program for students is documented by the recent CTS outcomes study. That study found that students who had participated in the internship program felt better prepared for ministry than students who had not participated in internship on eleven out of eleven categories (at a $p < .01$ level of significance).[18] (No other variable yielded statistically significant findings in more than five categories at $p < .05$ levels!) This astounding finding, together with the strong affirmation of the internship program by Alliance congregations, is eloquent testimony to the partnership between the institution and its churches.

Doctor of Ministries Program Encouraged
by Denominational Leaders

A second evidence of attentiveness to its constituent church is the CTS doctor of ministries (D.Min.) program. In the early 1980s the administration of CTS was encouraged by denominational leaders to initiate a D.Min. program. When a Director of Continuing Education was appointed in 1985, the seminary was ready to accept this challenge. To enable the seminary to launch the program by the fall of 1987, each of the four Anglophone districts of the C&MA allocated $6000 for start-up money. Since these grants came from district funds, they testify again to the pattern of responsiveness and affirmation which exists between CBC/CTS and its constituent church.

Curriculum Review Seeking Pastoral Input

The approach of CBC to its 1986 curriculum review and revision affords further evidence of the institution's attentiveness to its church.

The curriculum changes introduced find their origins in a spiritual pilgrimage of the faculty begun in the early 1980s. Out of this came a desire to make school chapel services occasions for meaningful worship and to see students growing in spirituality. The faculty also was conscious that the demands of pastoral ministry change with each generation and was committed to draw Alliance pastors into the curriculum development process.

When the decision was made to review the curriculum, letters were sent to a select list of nearly 100 Alliance pastors (in a denomination of fewer than 300 churches), soliciting advice regarding training needed for church ministries. Responses were collated and used by the faculty to draft a proposed curriculum. This curriculum draft was distributed to the same list of pastors with a request for feedback and suggestions. Again, responses were analyzed and further revisions made before the new curriculum was adopted. That curriculum, which includes a four-year spiritual formation track and a skills-and-knowledge approach to Bible instruction, reflects clearly the dynamic interaction of the faculty and church in its development.

Leadership Training for Denominational Church Planting Thrust

Another demonstration of CBC/CTS's attentiveness to its church is seen in the launching in 1984 of Enseignement Theologique de L'Alliance au Quebec (ETAQ). Early in the 1980s the president of the Alliance requested the assistance of the college in addressing leadership training support for a denominational church planting thrust in Quebec. The institution's response was to open an extension of the college's program in Quebec, with faculty appointed from Regina. During the 1987-88 school year sixty-six students enrolled in the ETAQ program.

Commitment to Seek Alternate Delivery Systems

CBC/CTS continues to be attentive to the needs of C&MA congregations across Canada. The institution has determined it will not allow unlimited growth of enrollment at its Regina campus but will seek to more adequately serve the church through alternate delivery systems and types of training. Currently the faculty and administration are reviewing a proposal to launch one or more "institutes," located in any of Canada's major cities, for training Alliance laity in specific fields of ministry. Since many Canadian young people attend Bible college for one year only, another proposal envisions one-year regional satellite programs which would meet the needs of those students and serve as a feeder system for the Regina campus. Although neither of these proposals may be adopted, they reflect the openness of the institution to the specific training needs of C&MA believers and their churches.

Factors Contributing to Church Attentiveness at CBC/CTS

It is tempting to suggest that a special relationship exists between CBC/CTS and its constituent church because these are denominational schools. That proposition is unproductive, at least, since few institutions are able to acquire or change church affiliation. More seriously, the assumption lacks power to account for the observed attentiveness. Other denominational institutions do not enjoy this relationship.

Benefits of the institution's denominational status, however, include:

- Precise identification of the church to be served.
  Although this is not a sufficient cause for the positive relationship observed, it is certainly a necessary condition.

- Strong mutual commitment existing between the institution and C&MA churches in Canada.

  CBC and CTS are the only schools of the C&MA in Canada, and the denomination looks to them as the principal source of its ministers. On the other hand, President Rose and most faculty (53% at CBC; 64% at CTS) have served as missionaries or ministers of the church.

- Open channels of communication.

Communication channels do not exist spontaneously. They must be cultivated and maintained. In this regard CBC/CTS has been fortunate to have a succession of presidents who have valued and pursued open communication with the church. When asked how he intends to address the challenges facing the institution today, President Rose responded by affirming his faith in God and his commitment to dialogue with the church.

Observations on Attentiveness to the Church

Interdenominational and nondenominational schools will particularly benefit from recognizing they cannot attend to the church until they first identify which church(es) they seek to serve. Although denominational institutions understand whom they serve, many interdenominational schools have never focused their attention on any specific segment of the Church. Clearly identifying a denomination or small group of denominations as the school's principal constituency does not preclude matriculation of students from other churches. CBC/CTS, like most denominational schools, has students from several denominations on its campus. What is important, however, is that an institution knows whom it seeks to serve. This allows it to focus its attentiveness and respond in meaningful ways to specific needs.

While other schools may not enjoy strong support from their constituent churches, commitment to the church is best grounded in a theological understanding of the centrality of the church in God's plan of redemption. Faculties seeking to be more attentive to the church may wish to explore a theological understanding of the church and ministry.

Ultimately, however, attentiveness to the church demands disciplined listening. Where channels of communication do not exist, the burden rests on theological educators—and particularly on administrators and boards of theological schools—to create opportunities for listening and dialogue. When communication is initiated by the church (as has been, on occasion, in the experience of CBC/CTS), theological educators have a priceless opportunity to demonstrate the genuineness of their commitment to listen and to serve.

Outcomes Assessment at CTS

Originally chartered in 1973 as Canadian Theological College, the current name of CTS was given royal assent after approval by the Saskatchewan Legislature on July 9, 1982. At that time the administration appointed a feasibility committee to study the appropriateness of applying for accreditation by the Association of Theological Schools in the United States and Canada (ATS). The committee concluded that the seminary was not ready to seek accreditation but recommended that the faculty proceed with a self-imposed program review modeled after an ATS "self-study." As part of that review, an initial outcomes study was undertaken.

In 1984, seminary graduates of 1972-1983 were polled using an instrument developed by CTS using sample questionnaires from Trinity Evangelical Divinity School and Dallas Theological Seminary, plus some original items. Prior to distribution, the instrument was tested with the graduates of 1984 and revised to replace open-ended items with closed-ended items, simplifying data analysis. The Seminary's alumni provided a 53% rate of response (145 of 275 survey instruments distributed). Initial findings were inconclusive, however, despite extensive computations.

In 1986, CTS professor of Christian education, Leslie Andrews, completed doctoral studies in educational administration and returned to CTS to assume the position of Director of Continuing Education. Under Andrews' direction, the outcomes survey was extended to graduates of 1984-86, and a new analysis of data was undertaken. This second analysis yielded highly useful findings, which were incorporated into a self study report submitted to ATS in 1988.

Design of the CTS Outcomes Study

The instrument developed for the CTS outcomes study consists of 214 items presented in three sections. Section I consists of sixteen demographic items (see Table 4.1).

TABLE 4.1

CTS Outcomes Survey
Section I: Demographic Items
(Independent Variables)

1. Year of graduation from CTS
2. Degree earned (i.e., academic program)
3. Age at time of graduation
4. Sex
5. Marital status during most of seminary years
6. Present marital status
7. Number of children at time of graduation
8. Average outside employment workload while a student
9. Principal field work experience while a student
10. Participation/non-participation in internship
11. Pre-seminary education
12. Highest degree earned after seminary
13. Cumulative grade point average in seminary
14. Present occupation (student/religious/secular)
15. Present religious vocation
16. Present salary range

Section II elicits the respondent's opinion of the adequacy of preparation for ministry at CTS using ninety-nine items covering eleven instructional fields. In Section III, the same ninety-nine items are repeated, this time requesting the respondent's opinion regarding the importance for ministry of the information, attitude, capacity, or skill identified in the item. The instructional fields represented in the instrument, as well as the distribution of items across those fields, are presented in Table 4.2. The instrument employed a five-point Likert-type scale of respondent opinion. The stimuli employed and the definition of response categories in Sections II and III of the instrument are presented in Table 4.3.

TABLE 4.2

CTS Outcomes Survey
Instructional Fields
(Dependent Variables)

Instructional Field	Total Items	Items Numbered
1. Theology	16	(1- 9,11,16,17,27,35,41,69)
2. Bible Knowledge	18	(6,10-26)
3. Church History	5	(27-29,31,40)
4. Missiology	16	(29-39,41,60,77-79)
5. Spiritual Formation	14	(42,44-52,56,94,98,99)
6. Interpersonal Relationships	4	(43,47,55,56)
7. Administration	8	(80,82-86,94,97)
8. Counseling	6	(55-60)
9. Pastoral Care	14	(61-68,76,78-80,95,96)
10. Teaching	5	(70-74)
11. Age Level Ministries	7	(87-93)

TABLE 4.3

Section II and III Stimuli and Response Categories

SECTION II: Measurement of Preparation for Ministry—

Stimulus: To what extent did Canadian Theological Seminary prepare you with the following areas of knowledge, attitudes, capacities, and skills for performing your ministries?

Response:

1 - Not at all (implies you were not prepared in this area)
2 - Poorly (implies you were prepared insufficiently)
3 - Fairly (implies you were somewhat prepared)
4 - Well (implies you were well prepared)
5 - Very well (implies you were prepared very well)

SECTION III: Measurement of Needs in Ministry—

Stimulus: As you view the work of the ministry today from your vantage point, how would you evaluate the need for the following areas of knowledge, attitudes, capacities, and skills to perform your ministries effectively?

Response:

1 - Not applicable (implies that your ministries do not require this kind of knowledge, ability, attitudes, capacities, and skills)
2 - Negligible need (implies that your ministries have little need for this kind of knowledge, etc.)
3 - Moderate need (implies that your ministries have somewhat of a need for this kind of knowledge, etc.)
4 - Significant need (implies that your ministries have a rather large need for this kind of knowledge, etc.)
5 - Extreme need (implies that your ministries have a maximum priority need for this kind of knowledge, etc.)

Data were analyzed using t-tests by creating sub-groups within the independent variables. (For example, data were grouped twice by G.P.A., first 2.00-3.00 vs. 3.01-4.00, then 2.00-3.50 vs. 3.51-4.00.) Correlations between adequacy of preparation and ministry needs for each variable were computed using Pearson's "r." A significance level for the study was established at $p \geq .05$. An interpretation of findings is presented in the body of the self study report (see sample interpretation in Table 4.4), supported by statistical tables in the report's appendices (see sample Table 4.5).

TABLE 4.4

Sample CTS Outcomes Survey Data Interpretation[19]

G.P.A. (Tables M-29, M-30, M-31, and M-32)

No significant differences were observed among subjects based on G.P.A.s of 2.00-3.00 (N=49) and G.P.A.s of 3.01-4.00 (N=119) at the time of graduation. (See Tables M-29 and M-31.)

When analyzed, however, on the basis of G.P.A.s of 2.00-3.50 (N=142) and 3.51-4.00 (N=26) at the time of graduation, significant differences [relative to ministry preparation—see Table M-30] were observed on two scales:

(1) Admin $(M_1 = 3.04, M_2 = 2.59, p = 0.018)$, and
(2) Pastoral $(M_1 = 2.90, M_2 = 2.41, p = 0.014)$.

Significance [relative to ministry preparation] was almost achieved on Bib Know $(p = 0.065)$ and Teaching $(p = 0.060)$.

No significant differences were observed among graduates relative to ministry needs along the eleven scales based upon G.P.A. (See Table M-32.)

Observations: In each instance, graduates with G.P.A.s of 2.00-3.50 felt better prepared for their ministries than did graduates with G.P.A.s of 3.51-4.00. Both administration and pastoral care are applied dimensions of theological education.

The findings may suggest that "function" is not highly correlated with cognitive ability and, therefore, those who "do" well in ministry may feel adequately prepared for the ministry. The findings are based on a limited sample, however, of "A" students (N=26) and, therefore, should be interpreted with caution.

Recommendation: That students earning higher G.P.A.s be counseled about the general need for such students to take elective courses in applied areas to balance more adequately their academic programs.

TABLE 4.5

Sample CTS Outcomes Survey Data Table[20]

TABLE 30. Preparation Outcomes for G.P.A.

Curriculum Component	3.51-4.00 (N=26)		2.00-3.50 (N=142)		Difference	t	p*
	M	SD	M	SD			
Theology 2.90	1.04	3.15	0.78	-0.254	1.439	0.148	
Bib Knowledge	2.43	1.15	2.90	0.90	-0.469	1.831	0.065
Church History	3.27	1.30	3.18	0.91	0.092	0.440	0.665
Missiology	2.77	1.02	2.97	0.91	-0.199	1.005	0.317
Spiritual Form	3.27	0.89	3.49	0.72	-0.212	1.332	0.181
Interpers Rel	3.28	0.92	3.56	0.77	-0.277	1.633	0.100
Administrat'n	2.59	0.88	3.04	0.87	-0.442	2.373	0.018
Counseling	3.03	1.06	3.23	0.96	-0.202	0.974	0.667
Pastoral	2.41	1.01	1.90	0.92	0.488	2.464	0.014
Teaching	2.81	1.15	3.21	0.98	-0.401	1.868	0.060
Age Level	2.55	1.10	2.82	1.03	-0.270	1.211	0.225

* p = 2-tailed.

Observations on the Use of Outcomes Studies

Initial impetus toward the use of an outcomes study at CTS came from the requirements for accreditation by ATS. Having completed a successful outcomes study, however, the Seminary is convinced of its value. Formal recommendations included in the self study report call for "an outcomes survey [to] be administered every five years..."[21]

Benefits derived from the outcomes study extended far beyond the curriculum implications of the findings. The survey of alumni communicated openness to the Seminary's alumni and built positive rapport. The exercise also sensitized faculty to curriculum questions they were not previously asking.

A successful study will be directed by a member of the faculty or staff who possesses the appropriate research skills. The critical difference between CTS's first outcomes study, with its inconclusive results, and the second, highly significant study was the arrival of a faculty person who had acquired educational research skills. At the same time, the seminary purchased a commercial software package to run statistical computations on a personal computer. Other institutions intending to conduct outcomes surveys would be wise to assure that the study is directed by someone with the requisite skills and with access to data processing technology.

As with all survey research, the design of the survey instrument will limit or expand the usefulness of the findings. Schools should not assume that they can obtain an instrument used by another institution. To the extent that the constituency, mission, educational philosophy, and curricula of two institutions differ, to the same extent useful instruments for surveying the educational outcomes of those institutions will also differ. Although the CTS faculty referred to other instruments in constructing their own, the instrument developed for this survey reflects the values and objectives of their institution.

Care should also be taken to assure that each variable in the study is assigned an appropriate distribution of items in the survey instrument. Since test statistics used in the CTS study compare mean scores of item responses, care should be taken to assure that each variable is represented by at least a minimum number of items (ideally, six to eight). The reliability of findings is threatened by item ambiguity and omitted responses when any variable is represented by a few items only.

In this study three variables received minimal representation in the survey instrument (Interpersonal relationships = 4 items; Church history = 5 items; and Counseling = 5 items). It is more important that each variable should be represented by sufficient, carefully selected, and well-framed items than that items should include a comprehensive list of training goals. A comprehensive representation of training goals would be appropriate, however, if the research design called for item-by-item (vs. mean score) analysis and interpretation.

Considering all these factors, the experience of the CTS outcomes study is still very encouraging. Most institutions can experience similar benefits. Schools with low felt need or high faculty work loads may benefit the most. Few experiences are more effective at opening a faculty to change and renewal than a well-designed and executed outcomes study. Those who desire renewal should consider carefully the advantages afforded.

Further Information

Requests for current information about CBC/CTS may be addressed to:

> Dr. Robert A. Rose, President
> Canadian Bible College and
> Canadian Theological Seminary
> 4400 Fourth Avenue
> Regina, SK, Canada   S4T 0H8
>
> Telephone: (306) 667-5811

CHAPTER 5

China Graduate School of Theology
Hong Kong

China Graduate School of Theology (CGST) is an Asian, graduate level, Cantonese language, ministry training institution which demonstrates cultural appropriateness and strategic flexibility. Clear evidence indicates that the Seminary has been committed to these values since the earliest discussions which led to its founding in 1975. Within its innovative programming, one can see evidence of other renewal values as well. CGST has excellent relations with other Asian seminaries through its leadership in Asia Theological Association and is highly regarded by evangelical churches and parachurch ministries in Hong Kong and among overseas Chinese.

Description of Ministry Training at CGST

It could reasonably be argued that CGST is a collection of three ministry training institutions, with its evening extension school and its unique program of ministry training for the basic stratum known as Jifu. As its name states, however, it is first and foremost a graduate school of theology.

Graduate School of Theology

The Seminary offers four graduate level programs, a one-year Diploma in Christian Studies (Dip.C.S.), a two-year Master of Christian Studies (M.C.S.), a three-year Master of Divinity (M.Div.), and a Master of Theology (Th.M.) program for post-M.Div. studies.

The M.C.S. and M.Div. programs each include areas of emphasis. M.C.S. students may choose among emphases in Biblical studies, theological and historical studies, or practical ministries. M.Div. students are offered emphases in pastoral ministries, counseling, and missions and evangelism. The Dip.C.S. program is offered in both day and evening formats, while the other three degrees are available through the daytime program only. Enrollment statistics indicate the M.Div. course is the centerpiece of CGST's training programs with more than two-thirds of all full-time students working towards that degree.[22]

CGST operates on a quarter system with courses offered during three quarters each year. Students enrolling in the graduate school must be university or Bible college graduates.

The staff of CGST often refer to three aspects of training—academic, practical work, and spiritual formation—and unsatisfactory development in any area can preclude granting of a degree by the Seminary.

CGST takes a multidimensional approach to spiritual formation for ministry, employing spiritual retreats, faculty advisory groups, chapel services, prayer days, and campus community life. Each school year is launched with a five-day spiritual retreat during which faculty and students gather for a time of Biblical messages, private meditation, and small group relationship building. During the retreat, assignment to faculty advisee groups is announced for the coming year. Each group consists of one faculty member and eight to ten students, and it is in these groups that discussion of message topics and relationship-building activities take place. A second, three-day retreat prior to the beginning of the third term allows students and faculty to assess (and, if necessary, reset) priorities for the final segment of the school year.

Faculty advisee groups function throughout the school year with weekly meetings provided in the Seminary schedule. Group activities oscillate between a thirty-minute prayer meeting on one week, and a ninety-minute sharing and discussion period on alternate weeks. In addition to scheduled meetings, advisee groups arrange informal activities which may include picnics, outings, or a party at the home of the faculty advisor. Students are interviewed annually by the Dean of Students, and faculty advisors are encouraged to schedule personal interviews with each member of their advisee group once each term.

Chapel services are held three days a week,[23] with focus given to sharing spiritual challenge and encouragement by members of the CGST community. Faculty are often slated as chapel speakers and are encouraged to share lessons from their own spiritual lives. New students are scheduled to give personal testimonies in chapel during the first term of each school year, and graduating M.Div. students are assigned to speak in chapel during the third term of their senior year.

Community life activities at CGST center on the campus where all single students and some married students are required to live. (Shortage of married family apartments precludes housing all married students on campus.) CGST requires living on campus out of a conviction that spiritual formation is profoundly affected by the daily interaction of community life. In the early years of the Seminary, when faculty and student populations were smaller, the faculty lived on campus with the students. This provided an invaluable context for sharing—and shaping—values and lifestyles. Today only one faculty family and one single member of the faculty still live on campus, although other faculty members regularly take their noon meal with students, and many take their evening meal in the campus dining room as well. Campus life activities are student organized and led, and often include prayer vigils, parties, and athletic competitions.

No practical work requirements per se are placed on first-year students, but they are encouraged to maintain involvement in their home church while adjusting to the academic rigors of graduate theological training. Beginning in the second year, students are required to engage in a practical work assignment. This means that M.Div. students receive two years of field education, while M.C.S. students receive only one year. Dip.C.S. students are not required to be involved in field education since the objectives of that program are limited to providing basic theological training for active lay churchmen.[24]

Since the Seminary receives many more requests for student workers than it can fill, the Office of Field Education can afford to select carefully the location for student placements. To be considered for placement, a church or parachurch agency must agree to provide meaningful activity for the student, plus responsible supervision of student ministry. Upon placement, the student and his or her ministry supervisor work out a ministry plan using a form developed by the Seminary (see Figure 5.1). When the ministry plan is submitted for approval by the CGST Director of Field Education, he notes the areas of ministry involvement, using a checklist included on the form, to assure the student receives appropriate exposure and opportunities for ministry skills development.

In addition to a ministry supervisor, each student's ministry experience is also overseen by his or her faculty advisor. The faculty advisor receives a copy of the Field Work Planning Sheet (see Figure 5.1), and students are required to submit to their faculty advisor and the Director of Field Education quarterly reports on their ministry involvement. Ministry supervisors are also required to submit semiannual reports on student involvement and ministry development, but difficulties are usually registered more quickly through phone contacts between the Office of Field Education and ministry supervisors. Lack of progress or problems in ministry become topics of discussion in the student's regular interviews with his or her faculty advisor. These may also be addressed in an interview with the Director of Field Education.

Figure 5.1

CGST Practical Work Planning Sheet

Date	Goal	Activities	Fellowship	Teaching	Worship	Preaching	Pastoral Care	Evangelism	Mission	Church Admin	Achievement

Agreed to by: Approved by:

_____   _____
(Student Worker)   CGST Director Of Field Education

_____
(Ministry Supervisor)

        M.C.S. and M.Div. students are also required to spend one summer
term (six weeks) in a full-time, supervised ministry assignment. Often
the summer ministry requirement is met following the first year of
study and lays the groundwork for more meaningful involvement in the

same ministry placement during the following school year. CGST prefers to place students in a local church for their summer ministry assignment but is sensitive to each student's gifts and sense of call to future ministry. Some very fruitful summer ministry placements have involved students in the work of parachurch agencies in Hong Kong, and the Seminary also has an active program of overseas, summer missionary placements.[25]

Students receive one unit of academic credit for each term they are engaged in a field education assignment.

Evening Extension School

The second major division of CGST's theological training ministries is its evening extension school.[26] The evening extension school offers a general program of theological training for lay leaders, plus two special two-year programs.

- A program for church leaders
  This program is designed to prepare lay leaders to lead small group (or cell group) meetings for Christian worship and nurture.

- A program for white collar workers
  This program aims to equip members of Hong Kong's business community to be effective witnesses and evangelists in their work places. The basic evening extension program does not follow a set curriculum but offers a variety of Biblical and theological courses, together with topical courses targeted at specific issues or challenges relevant to the Hong Kong setting.[27]

Evening extension courses currently are offered on the CGST campus and at two other locations in the city. Minimum entrance requirements for the evening extension school specify Form Five (eleventh grade) completion, but a majority of those enrolling are actually professionals. Students may receive a certificate of completion for each subject taken through the evening extension program, but no other certificate, diploma, or degree is offered.

Jifu School

The third major program of CGST is its "Jifu School"—a creative, three-year program designed to provide leadership training to members of the basic stratum, for ministry in and to the basic stratum.[28] This program has several distinctive features.

1) Unique mix of classroom activities—Because the basic stratum is made up of people who are oriented to action rather than academic studies or thinking, the Jifu program employs a unique mix of classroom activities with a heavy stress on team work and ministry involvement. Since most of the tutors involved in the Jifu program come from the basic stratum, instruction often takes the form of telling the Christian story through role play, case studies, and simulations. Bible doctrine is taught by developing themes embedded in the Lord's prayer. All classes make provision for extensive discussion of the truths studied and their meaning for life in the basic stratum.

2) Guided practicums—Biblical and ministry skill subjects are constantly related to and illustrated from experiences students encounter in guided practicums. During the first term of the program, practicums focus on basic evangelism, with students assigned in teams to witness to the families of team members and engage in street evangelism. Practicums during the second and third terms of the first year take students into evangelistic outreach as part of church planting teams. During the second year of Jifu training, students engage in extensive discipleship, devoting two to three days each week to following up those who have made a commitment to Christ. By the third year of the program, Jifu students are assigned to lead a church planting team in a factory, a housing estate, or an urban block. First-year Jifu students gain much of their evangelistic outreach experience by serving on these teams, while third-year students acquire organizational and leadership experience under the guidance of a faculty advisor.

Because the Jifu program runs year around, the three-year course comprises eleven quarters. Ten quarters are devoted to classroom and practicum activities, but one quarter (the eighth) is given to full-time ministry in an internship setting. Although one group of Jifu students recently spent their internship in an industrial mission in Singapore, it is more usual for students to work with churches or parachurch agencies ministering to the basic stratum in Hong Kong.

3) Personal Counseling—the Jifu program has a strong emphasis on personal counseling and growth groups. Because students are often scarred by past personal and family experiences, it is essential that problems are brought to the surface and dealt with so that inner healing can take place. Weekly group discussions focus on basic principles of the Christian life during the first year of training.[29] In the second year, the focus shifts to Christian patterns of personal and family life. Topics related to the Christian worker's resources in ministry assume priority during the final year of the program, with consideration given to mission and practice, meditation on Christ, and the worker's life of faith.

To avoid dislocation from the basic stratum, first-year students live at home with their families and commute to class. Currently second- and third-year students are required to live in a Jifu dormitory to experience Christian community life, but that may be reduced to one-and-a-half years so students can make the transition back into ministry contexts while they still have access to the support structures of the Jifu program.

The entire Jifu curriculum is highly integrated and sharply focused on developing evangelists and church planters for the basic stratum. Theory is minimized and emphasis is given to transferring models which students can directly implement in new ministry contexts. Because of the high level of student-teacher involvement, and because the pool of potential students is relatively small, Jifu only admits students on alternate years. This means that faculty can concentrate their attention on second-year students during discipleship training, and first- and third-year students can work together on evangelistic and church planting teams.

The most recent program to be opened at CGST extends training for the basic stratum to part-time lay students through an evening school format. This program, referred to as Jixuan, is currently structured as a three-year course, meeting two evenings per week. On the basis of the first two years' experience, however, the program is due to be restructured to incorporate a field work component. It is projected that two evenings per week will continue to be given to classroom activities, while two other evenings per week will be spent in field work. For their field work, Jixuan students will be assigned to work under the supervision of Jifu graduates. By restructuring the program in this way, completion time can be cut to one-and-a-half years.

Factors Contributing to the Development of CGST's Approach to Ministry Training

CGST does not have a long history, but factors contributing to the development of current programs preceded the opening of classes by at least ten years. In the mid-1960s, a handful of Chinese university students studying in the United States committed themselves to found a graduate level seminary to serve Chinese churches. Four elements were essential to that vision. The school was to be:

1) interdenominational in scope
2) evangelical in commitment
3) graduate level in instruction
4) indigenous in orientation and development

The tenacious commitment of these students can only be appreciated by understanding that each of the original four pursued that vision through university and seminary training, and on to completion of Ph.D. or Th.D. studies in the U.S. Throughout these years of training, the men maintained monthly contact with one another, sharing observations from their areas of study and noting strengths and weaknesses in western educational systems.

In 1969 the band obtained a grant from Liberty Foundation and convened a Consultation on Chinese Theological Education. Speakers invited to address the consultation were drawn from America's best-known evangelical theological educators, including Carl F.H. Henry, Kenneth Kantzer, Arthur Glasser, and Paul Rees. Principles shared by these leaders helped to shape the maturing vision for a Chinese seminary.

The Lord blessed the group with dynamic and visionary leadership from Jonathan Chao—a man who has written prolifically, has since established the Chinese Church Research Center, China Mission Seminary, and China Ministries International, and whose influence is evident in several Christian ministries in Hong Kong, Taiwan, and North America.

Each member of the group seized every opportunity to equip himself for the challenge of opening a seminary for China. In 1968, when Rev. David Adeney, leader of Overseas Missionary Fellowship, established Discipleship Training Center in Singapore, Che-Bin Tan, another member of the original group, was at his side, observing and learning from Adeney's example. Two years later, when Dr. James Taylor launched China Evangelical Seminary in Taiwan, Che-Bin Tan and Jonathan Chao were also part of that operation. In the meantime, the band had added Peter Chang, a young man whose studies were to take him to Strasbourg, France, for a doctorate in New Testament and on to Michigan State University for postdoctoral work in nonformal education. Throughout this period the monthly letters continued to flow, carrying reflections on each one's educational experiences and the needs of Chinese churches.

A second Consultation on Chinese Theological Education was held in Hong Kong in 1972, but the participants in this consultation were Chinese theological educators, and the thrust of the consultation was to build a consensus on the need for graduate level ministry training for the Chinese church. During the consultation the Association for Promotion of Chinese Theological Education (APCTE) was founded with Philip Teng as Chairman and Jonathan Chao as Executive Secretary. The Association sponsored a follow-up conference in Baguio City, Philippines, the following year which focused on "Church Growth and Theological Education." The result of these meetings was to develop a network of Chinese educators and pastors who were committed to join hands in united support for a graduate level Chinese seminary.

In 1973 two of the men moved to Hong Kong, but the time for launching the seminary they had dreamed of was not yet ripe. First they made a thorough study of the curricula of all evangelical ministry training institutions in Hong Kong, noting the strengths of each. The men were committed to do things "properly" from the beginning, so a formal catalog was published outlining the courses of study and stating the academic qualifications of each instructor. Finally, in 1975, the first class of students was admitted.

God's grace is also evident in the willingness of Dr. Philip Teng to serve as the first president of the new seminary. President Teng is a widely recognized and highly regarded leader among Protestant Chinese churches world wide, and his association with the fledgling seminary provided immediate credibility. More important, however, he possessed the unique capacity to create an atmosphere of freedom for experimentation by the faculty while maintaining a sensitive awareness of the context in which they worked.

Another individual who exerted a profound influence on the development of training programs at CGST is the Board Chairman, Dr. Philemon Choi. Dr. Choi is a man of considerable sensitivity and talent, evidenced in his role as General Secretary of Breakthrough, a Christian youth ministry with extensive counseling, publication, and media production divisions. Through his personal investment in the lives of CGST faculty and administrators he has raised awareness of the central role of personal wholeness in preparation for ministry. Most counseling courses at CGST are taught by Dr. Choi or members of the Breakthrough staff, and much of the small group activity included in CGST training programs owes its inspiration to his influence.

Other influences have come as well. In 1980 Dr. Peter Chang was approached by the leaders of Hong Kong's Industrial Evangelistic Fellowship, Wu Oi (an evangelical drug abuse rehabilitation program), and the Methodist Epworth Village Community Center. Close collaboration with these organizations was extremely useful in developing the Jifu program.

Dr. Wilson Chow, long-term Dean of CGST and now President, has enjoyed international exposure and involvement through Asia Theological Association and the Theological Commission of World Evangelical Fellowship. These positions have taken Dr. Chow to conferences and consultations around the world, enabling him to learn from others while articulating clearly the need for biblically sound and contextually relevant ministry training for all churches.

Over and above these historical factors, several qualities stand out in any attempt to understand the organizational and intellectual milieu which has given rise to CGST's programs.

1) The high standards the Seminary has set for itself from the beginning. The resolve of the founders to delay launching the school until they could field a team of Chinese instructors with earned doctorates reflects this commitment. The care and patience taken to cultivate understanding and support among leaders of the evangelical Chinese community also had a profound effect. It is noteworthy, also, that the support of the Seminary is totally underwritten by Chinese churches. The resulting credibility the Seminary has enjoyed from its early days contributed to a context of personal and institutional security which made innovation acceptable.

2) Clear sense of commitment to the Chinese church. President Wilson Chow describes CGST as both an institution and a movement. The Seminary exists as an institution, but its objective is to effect renewal of the Chinese church and its worldwide mission. Speaking graphically, he compares the ecclesiastical and institutional dimensions of CGST's mission to a circle and its center. In order to draw a good circle, the center must be firmly established; but the purpose is not to elaborate the center, it is to draw the circle. This outward looking vision of the CGST staff has provided motivation and energy to sustain its drive for excellence on the one hand, and contextual relevance on the other.

3) Sense of mission. This is strengthened and supported by a community of shared values regarding the church, the ministry, and ministry training. The church must be solidly Biblical and authentically Chinese. Ministry must be spiritually vibrant and intellectually credible. And ministry training, therefore—in its content and structures— must be excellent, holistic, and relevant to the Chinese context.

4) A context of open dialogue and team spirit among the faculty. The Seminary is not dominated by a single leader who appears to embody all spiritual gifts, nor is it a collection of isolated professionals, each interested only in his or her own limited domain of expertise. Members of the staff are careful to share the things they learn in their respective areas of study, and are quick to learn from one another. They also are diligent in bringing their various disciplines to bear on specific issues facing the Church in Hong Kong. Each year the faculty conducts a public seminar for Christians in the city in which they address, from different perspectives, one issue of the day.[30]

5) Highly competent, extremely creative personnel, and an environment that encourages innovation. This combination, in a context of vision, commitment, and security, has enabled CGST to respond to training needs of the Christian community in Hong Kong with programs which are both appropriate and relevant.

Comments

The observation will come late to benefit most readers, but CGST clearly demonstrates that care in beginning an institution is worth the effort. The patient, thorough, methodical process by which this institution was launched goes far toward explaining the high reputation it enjoys today among Chinese churches in Hong Kong and abroad. Perhaps the lesson to be learned has application to other situations as well. Even new programs—especially when they seek to serve a new audience or incorporate innovative learning strategies—can expect a better reception and greater effectiveness if care is taken to cultivate understanding and confidence, as well as to assure the appropriateness of the program's design.

It is common wisdom that clarity of institutional focus provides direction for program development. CGST effectively demonstrates this principle. The early resolve that the Seminary should be interdenominational, evangelical, graduate, and indigenously Chinese has controlled the development of the Seminary and its programs. The institution's commitment to serve the Chinese church, articulated in President Chow's illustration of a circle and its center, has provided rationale and guidance in developing the Seminary's evening extension school and Jifu programs. The same sense of institutional focus is currently sparking discussion of opening a continuing education program to serve Hong Kong's pastoral community. It is encouraging to observe that the Seminary is not simply proliferating programs, however, but that program development has consistently been disciplined by the commitments of the institution. In this area, too, CGST provides a model other institutions may find helpful.

Administrators of theological schools may well be reminded by CGST's example that they determine the quality and tone of the institutional environment which, in turn, directly affects the attitudes and productivity of their instructional staff. Who would suggest that CGST could be the institution it is today if it were not for the early leadership of Jonathan Chao, the wise and supportive guidance of President Philip Teng, or the steady administrative hand of Dean (and now, President) Wilson Chow? Running a school is never a one-person operation, but someone must set the tone of the institution. If the president or principal defaults in this responsibility, someone else will pick up that role. When that occurs, many examples could be cited to indicate the end result may be unacceptable to the administrator or detrimental to the school.

Finally, one observing CGST must note that a clear institutional commitment to serve the Church, plus a context which encourages creativity and teamwork, is highly productive. Few graduate level seminaries are prepared to acknowledge they have a responsibility to provide ministry training for the basic stratum, and fewer still could create a program as non-traditional and contextually relevant as CGST's Jifu school. The Seminary certainly has outstanding personnel, but other seminaries and theological schools also have capable professionals. Perhaps what others lack (and might well seek to develop) is the combination of sensitivity and freedom which exists at CGST—sensitivity to the Church and its training needs, and freedom to experiment with non-traditional training models.

Further Information

Requests for current information about CGST may be addressed to:

Dr. Wilson Chow, President
China Graduate School of Theology
5 Devon Road, Kowloon Tong
Hong Kong

Telephone: (852-3) 374-106

CHAPTER 6

Columbia Bible College and Seminary

Columbia, South Carolina, U.S.A.

Columbia Bible College and Seminary (CBCS) is a non-denominational North American undergraduate and graduate ministry training institution which demonstrates flexible strategizing and spiritual formation. Because of the distinctive missionary emphasis of the institution, spiritual formation at CBCS incorporates a clear focus on cross-cultural evangelism.

Columbia Bible College (CBC), the undergraduate division of CBCS, and the graduate division, Columbia Biblical Seminary and Graduate School of Missions (CBS), share a common commitment—"To know Him, and to make Him known." This study will focus on strategic flexibility and spiritual formation; other aspects of the institution's training program also are important to the goals and ministries of CBCS.[31]

Evidence of Strategic Flexibility at CBCS

Strategic flexibility refers to an institution's sensitivity to training needs existing in the constituent church, and creativity in responding to those needs. Although CBCS has not formally identified a single church or group of churches as its primary constituency, the school has demonstrated a high level of sensitivity to training needs of evangelical Christians—especially those committed to world evangelism. This sensitivity, combined with creative restructuring of the institution's instructional programs, has resulted in a variety of undergraduate and graduate courses for world Christians.

Students entering CBC can currently elect to register for a one-year Bible Certificate, a two-year Associate of Arts, or four-year Bachelor of Arts program. All students in the bachelor's program major in Bible, with minors available in missions, pastoral ministries, Church music,

Christian education, Bible teaching, and pre-seminary studies. Double majors are also offered in Bible and missions, and in Bible and elementary education. In conjunction with one of the listed programs, students may also complete requirements for a certificate in Teaching English as a Second Language (TESL).

Students entering CBS also have an array of training options. The Seminary offers a three-track approach to ministry preparation, tailored to the needs of various students. The needs of college or university graduates who have not had formal biblical instruction are addressed in Program I. The prior training of Bible college graduates is recognized curricularly in Program II. And mature Christian workers who have at least three years of undergraduate Bible education may be admitted to Program III.

Within Programs I and II, seminary students may prepare for North American or cross-cultural overseas ministries at the M.A. or M.Div. level in pastoral studies, church planting, missions, Christian education, or evangelism. Program I also includes a Certificate in Biblical Studies which is designed, "To satisfy a mission agency requirement for one year of Bible/missions preparation." Program III students are limited to an M.A. curriculum, with concentrations in English, Bible or missions. Like their undergraduate counterparts, CBS students may also complete requirements for a certificate in Teaching English as a Second Language (TESL).

To meet the needs of students who find it difficult or impossible to come to the CBCS campus, the school offers correspondence courses through its extension division, Columbia School of Biblical Education (CSBE). While CSBE is not a degree granting division of CBCS, courses completed through the School of Biblical Extension may be credited toward undergraduate or graduate degree programs at Columbia. Currently, nearly 9000 students around the world are enrolled in CSBE.

Factors Contributing to Strategic Flexibility In Ministry Training at CBCS

The breadth of training options reported above reflects much more than a simple proliferation of programs, as evidenced by the enrollment statistics of the institution. In a period of generally declining Bible college enrollments, CBC's student population defied national trends through the 1985-86 school year. Enrollments did drop in 1986 and 1987 but have increased again in 1988. CBS, on the other hand, has grown at an astounding rate—from 65 students in 1972 to 420 in 1988! Although enrollment is not a reliable index of institutional effectiveness, these data indicate that CBCS is perceived by its constituency to be addressing significant training needs. Five factors, at least, must be considered in any attempt to understand CBCS's strategic flexibility over the past 20 years.

Clarity of Mission

First and foremost is the institution's sense of mission. The school motto, "To know Him, and to make Him known," is the touchstone for every aspect of the institution's programs. The first phrase of the motto— "To know Him"—furthermore, is always understood in terms of the second. Thus the institution values personal spirituality (see the discussion of spiritual formation below), but always within the context of mission. It is not accidental (as we shall see) that 32% of CBC faculty and 45% of CBS faculty are former missionaries. When CBCS adopted an institutional mission statement in 1985, therefore, it was appropriate that world missions should be prominent. The mission statement reads:

The mission of Columbia Bible College is to glorify God by assisting the church to evangelize the world in this generation, through helping God's people grow in spiritual maturity, Bible knowledge, and ministry skills.[32]

It is not difficult to recognize the impact of this commitment to world missions in the various programs offered by CBS. Although CBC offers a wider variety of programs as "minors," the missions emphasis is everywhere evident. Informal conversations with CBC and CBS students indicate that the missions emphasis of the institution was a dominant factor in student selection of CBCS as a place of preparation for ministry. Students also express uniform appreciation for the missions focus of their experience at CBCS, both in classes on cross-cultural ministry and throughout the curricula. Thus the institution's sense of mission—linked as it is with world evangelization—has provided both direction and incentive toward development of the programs currently offered.

Administrative Creativity

Integrally related to CBCS's sense of institutional mission is a commitment to creative responsiveness at the highest level of the school's administration. Dr. Robertson McQuilkin is the school's third president, having held that position since 1968. As a leader he exhibits creativity in dealing with challenges and is open to visionary and responsible suggestions from others.

An illustration of this is seen in a document currently under development within CBCS, titled "Vision 2000." Like many other organizations, CBCS has undertaken institutional planning looking toward the end of this century. Originally drafted by President McQuilkin and revised through successive review by members of the administration, faculty, and board, the "Vision 2000" statement is sweeping in scope. Quite apart from the challenges of implementing such a vision, this statement reflects an administration which is able to think grandly and is unafraid to do so. This capacity obviously has contributed to the strategic flexibility evident in the institution's curricular offerings.

Other illustrations of administrative creativity can be cited as well. Formation of the school's extension division, Columbia School of Biblical Education (CSBE), represents a creative response to the training needs of students—many of whom are overseas missionaries—who can only be served through distance education. The administration also is exploring development of linkages with overseas training institutions for the benefit of students of both schools.

Selection of Personnel

A clear sense of institutional mission and an innovative executive officer does not assure a context of organizational responsiveness and creativity, however. A third factor contributing to strategic flexibility at CBCS is careful selection of personnel who are committed to the institution's mission and who also are open and creative.

Four years passed between the appointment of McQuilkin as president in 1968, and appointment of Dr. Terry Hulbert as dean of the graduate school in 1972. During those years McQuilkin looked for a person who shared the institution's values, had a background in missions, and was an experienced academic administrator.

The care taken in making that appointment proved wise, however, when Hulbert immediately identified the need of missionary candidates for a one-year program in Bible and missions. The restructuring of the Seminary's curricular offerings which took place at the time of Hulbert's appointment laid the foundation for rapid expansion of graduate enrollments in the years that followed. Two men cannot produce a context of creative responsiveness, however, any more than one alone. In this regard, Hulbert's selection and appointment is representative of the deliberateness with which the CBCS administration and faculty have been built. The strategic flexibility of the institution is easier to understand when one recognizes the priority assigned to developing a team characterized by openness and creativity.

Attentiveness to Evaluation and Research

A fourth factor which informs and disciplines the CBCS administration's response to opportunities and challenges is attention to careful and responsible research. It is significant in this regard that McQuilkin has appointed an Assistant to the President whose principal assignment is institutional research and planning. Just as important, perhaps, is the presence of others in CBCS who have engaged in educational research. At least six faculty and administrators have completed research degrees in educational administration.[33]

A ready illustration of the administration's use of research to inform decision making is provided by the on-going challenge to maintain a viable Bible college program. Despite the encouraging performance of CBC for most of its history, nationwide patterns of Bible college enrollment have raised grave concern. When the enrollment of CBC turned down in 1986 and 1987, McQuilkin established a blue-ribbon "Commission on the Future of the Bible College." The Commission collected and reviewed data relevant to its task and prepared a report.[34] Eleven of the Commission's twelve recommendations on CBC's programs, operations, and facilities included in the report have been approved for implementation. This reflects the regard for and use of research within the CBCS administration.

Prayer

The last factor to be mentioned is one of the most important. The administration of this institution is committed to prayerful petition and intercession regarding the mission it bears and the challenges it faces. Openness before God in seeking his direction translates directly into openness to strategic adaptability and urgency in pursuing those responses which are seen as God's direction.

CBCS's Approach to Spiritual Formation

In an effort to take seriously a commitment to "whole life training," the administration of CBCS speaks of a programmatic "triad." The expression refers to the three elements of training identified in the institution's mission statement—"spiritual maturity, Bible knowledge, and ministry skills." The administration of the institution has recently been restructured to place these functions on more equal footing. Cultivating in students a knowledge of the Bible and an intellectual preparedness for ministry is the assignment of the academic division; training in ministry skills is assigned to the Ministry Development Division; and spiritual formation is the responsibility of the Student Affairs Division.

The Student Affairs Division is headed by a dean of student affairs and staffed with associate deans for men, women, and off-campus students. Students living in dormitories are supervised through a conventional structure of resident advisors and floor leaders. Parallel to this structure is a network of student-led small groups which meet at least weekly for personal sharing and prayer. The Student Affairs office assigns students to groups of six to ten persons by living units or geographical proximity and appoints a group leader. Student leaders are selected for their spiritual maturity and leadership and are provided with a basic orientation to the goals of the program. Direction of the group and formation of any agenda of topics to be discussed, however, is left to the leader and the group itself.

In addition to normal pastoral and counseling relationships, the Student Affairs Office evaluates the spiritual development of each student near the end of the second year of study. The student completes a self-assessment, using a prepared form. Each student's responses are reviewed by an associate dean, and any student who does not appear to be developing satisfactorily is referred to a faculty counselor. Advancement to upper division status is contingent on a positive recommendation by the faculty counselor. Approximately 25% to 30% of students each year are provided with personal counseling through this procedure.

Factors Contributing to Spiritual Formation At CBCS

The factor which is most striking about spiritual formation at CBCS is the contrast between the ordinariness of the systems employed and the extraordinariness of the result. Many theological schools have more elaborate systems for spiritual formation with less satisfactory effect. Two factors seem to account for the success of CBCS in developing Christian disciplines and inculcating spiritual values.

Faculty Selection

Those familiar with CBCS often associate the spiritual effect of the institution on students with an "ethos" which pervades the campus. On closer observation it becomes clear that this ethos constitutes the shared values and lifestyle of the school's administration and faculty. The depth of commitment to the institution's mission and the consistency of spiritual fervor among faculty reflects, in turn, the approach taken to personnel procurement.

The Academic Dean of CBC, without introduction or context, was asked in an interview what he looks for in a potential faculty person. His first response was that he seeks a person of deep spiritual commitment. In his terms, the spiritual qualification of the potential candidate forms "the first screen." He granted that academic preparation is important but pointed out that many persons with excellent academic credentials are seeking teaching positions today. He noted that the college prefers a candidate with prior teaching experience and demonstrated competence, and commented that successful missionary experience is appreciated. He reaffirmed, however, that his first consideration is spiritual maturity.

The procedure employed at CBCS for faculty selection provides ample opportunity for the administration to assess the suitability of candidates and effectively guard the values of the institution. When a faculty search is undertaken, the administration prefers to initiate contact with persons viewed as potential candidates, rather than announce the opening. Those who are open to possible appointment are provided with a standard application form which includes a request for four references. These are followed up, including a request for each reference to identify three additional references. The CBCS administration has found that these secondary references are often the most helpful in providing an objective perspective on the candidate and identifying areas of potential concern. If the application procedure is encouraging, the candidate is invited to visit campus with his or her spouse for a more personal exchange in face-to-face interviews with CBCS administrators. At this time the president meets with the candidate and spouse, thus taking a direct role in the selection process. Subsequent to the visit, a decision is made by the CBCS administrators, sitting as a cabinet, as to the appropriateness of inviting the candidate to join the faculty.

When asked why such a rigorous approach is taken to faculty selection, the dean responded that the administration is convinced this is necessary for two reasons. First, careful faculty selection is essential to guard the values of the institution. Since the faculty of any school, in effect, are the institution, inclusion of faculty who do not share the school's values can only undermine and, in time, alter those values. Second, CBCS is committed to an educational philosophy which is holistic, embracing thought and life, so that faculty are expected to model in their personal, family, and professional life the truths which they teach. Modeling is never absent. If faculty do not model consistency of faith and life, they certainly model an inconsistency which is detrimental to the mission of CBCS as a training institution.

Institutional Emphasis on Spirituality, Missions, and Prayer

In addition to the informal modeling provided by the faculty, an emphasis on spirituality, missions, and prayer is communicated at CBCS through programmatic structures and institutional response.

Until recently, McQuilkin annually taught first-year courses at both undergraduate and graduate levels on "Christian Living." Drawing from the theological heritage of the Keswick tradition, in this course the president set a tone for the campus which holds victorious living as the normal Christian life. First-year students also enroll in an "Introduction to Missions" course which challenges them to be world Christians. Bible classes throughout the curriculum teach and demonstrate a hermeneutic which emphasizes obedience to the Word as an integral part of right understanding.

At a time when many Bible schools and seminaries have shortened chapel periods or replaced daily chapel with a less frequent schedule, CBCS has recently lengthened its daily chapel time to a full sixty minutes. When asked why this was done, the president pointed to the need for corporate prayer. Under the present schedule, prayer chapels are scheduled weekly.

Another material demonstration of the institution's commitment to prayer is the construction in 1987 of a prayer tower on campus. This beautifully designed and appointed brick structure, set in wooded seclusion on the edge of campus, is in constant use by students and faculty. When asked to explain the source of spiritual emphasis on campus, one graduate student pointed to the prayer tower. At his undergraduate Bible college, he reported, students had a difficult time convincing the administration to set aside a closet as a prayer room. At CBCS, in contrast, the administration constructed a prayer tower. Procurement of scarce assets for this use communicates a powerful message to students.

Commitment of the CBCS administration to spirituality, world missions, and prayer is also evidenced in the financial operation of the institution. Unlike many theological schools which receive regular allocations from denominational budgets or have built up substantial endowments, CBCS has chosen to follow a "faith mission" principle for campus development and general operating funds. The administration is not opposed to endowments in principle—in fact the school holds a small endowment (about $1 million) for student scholarships and would like to enlarge it.

On the other hand, they find it helpful to live in monthly dependence upon the Lord to provide contributions needed for operations and salaries. Tuition income covers about 70% of what is needed, but the balance must come from gifts. Within the past year the CBCS community has gathered to pray for God's provision, and faculty have taken salary prorations when funds have been low. Together students and faculty also have rejoiced as God has answered prayer, enabling the school to restore the full amount of salaries cut. The administration is convinced that this demonstration of dependence upon God and his faithfulness provides a model which encourages students called to a life of faith.

Observations

Theological schools seeking renewal can learn much about strategic flexibility and spiritual formation from the CBCS approach to ministry training. One message which comes through very clearly is the critical role of the chief executive officer. Few schools will be prepared to change presidents or principals to enhance institutional effectiveness, although some would benefit from such courage. Boards of control and the faculties they consult should not miss the point, however, that selection of a chief executive officer may well be the most important single action the board will consider. In addition, continuity of administrative leadership is a great benefit.

For chief executive officers, the lesson in this case is equally clear. Through personal creativity and openness, one can set the tone for a faculty and an administration. When the warmth of one's own spiritual life is brought to bear on an institution, furthermore, it can have a shaping effect on the lives of generations of students. This is both a great encouragement and a great challenge.

Other principles are more easily transferred. Clarification of institutional mission is essential to effectiveness. CBCS's focus on preparing men and women to be world Christians has been most significant.

It is also clear that careful selection of personnel is the key to preserving institutional values and achieving training objectives. Many administrators have had occasion to regret staffing decisions which focused too narrowly on technical qualifications. CBCS demonstrates the wisdom of broadly-considered personnel decisions.

Again, the modeling effect of an institution's chief executive officer and faculty shapes the administrative and instructional context which guides the life of the school. This simply may be a different way of saying the same thing—by appointing a president and faculty, the nature of a school is determined. The lesson is so basic, yet so profound.

Schools which already employ a staff researcher within their administration will understand the clarity which hard data can provide for decision making. Other schools may want to consider designating a faculty person with an interest in quantitative and organizational research to serve part-time in this capacity. Even when a regular appointment is impossible, temporary research teams can be assigned to gather and analyze data relative to major administrative and policy decisions. Ongoing evaluation of institutional training and outcomes, as well as research on administrative challenges, does not eliminate the need for careful (and prayerful) leadership. Systematic evaluation and research, however, can provide an invaluable foundation for responsible decision making. Schools which historically have relied on an intuitive approach to administration would be wise to consider a research-based alternative.

All evangelical theological educators advocate priority on prayer as a discipline of the Christian life and acknowledge its centrality in preparation for ministry. Unfortunately, that commitment is not evidenced in the programs of many theological education institutions. Including occasions for prayer (through prayer days, frequent prayer chapels, prayer rooms, etc.) is both essential and insufficient. Only as faculty and administrators are men and women of prayer can they expect to see the power of prayer evidenced on their campuses and through their students.

Finally, the particular institutional emphasis at CBCS on spirituality, mission, and prayer may be attractive to other ministry training institutions as well. It cannot be denied that the three emphases support and reinforce each other. Other ways to foster these commitments certainly exist, and theological educators will want to explore patterns which reflect their own institutional values and style. Where spiritual formation is valued, however, such an emphasis at an institutional level bears a great impact on student development. Some administrators may want to examine the emphases which characterize their campus and reflect on the role that these play in shaping students.

Further Information

Requests for current information about CBCS may be addressed to:

Dr. Robertson McQuilkin, President
Columbia Bible College and Seminary
Post Office Box 3122
Columbia, SC 29230

Telephone: (803) 754-4100

CHAPTER 7

Jos ECWA Theological Seminary
Jos, Nigeria

Jos ECWA Theological Seminary (JETS) is a four-year Bible college[35] located in Jos, Plateau State, Nigeria, serving the Evangelical Churches of West Africa (ECWA). The school demonstrates cultural appropriateness and flexible strategizing.

Description of Ministry Training at JETS

JETS offers students the B.A. degree with majors in pastoral ministries, teaching ministries, and communications ministries. Admission to JETS is granted by the faculty Admissions Committee upon submission of application documents and references, and a personal interview. Academic standards for admission to JETS are standard Nigerian university entrance qualifications.

At the time of application, the student is required to declare the major for which he or she is applying. In response to perceived needs in the constituent church, the college has established a goal for distribution of majors among students admitted in each entering class. Ideally, the school would like 60% of each class admitted to major in pastoral ministries, 25% in teaching ministries, and 15% in communications ministries. Registration statistics indicate, however, that these ideals are not always attainable.[36]

During the first year of study, each student is required to meet with the Academic Dean, who reviews the student's previous training and experience. At that time the Dean makes any indicated adjustments in the student's curriculum. In this way the school's academic administration intends to assure congruency between each student's training needs and the training provided through the program in which he or she is enrolled.

Each major includes courses which attend specifically to the school's Nigerian context. Courses such as "Third World Theologies," "Socio-Political African Problems," "Western and Non-Western Thought," and "Islamic Law" illustrate the seriousness with which the faculty has taken the challenge to contextualize instruction at JETS.

Even more important, however, is the cultural perspective from which all courses in the curriculum are taught. To assure implementation of the Seminary's commitment to contextualization, all lecturers are required to submit to the Dean a copy of their syllabi at the beginning of each term, with indication of specific incorporation of African perspectives.

Classroom courses are supplemented with a program of field education, faculty advisement, and personal discipleship on campus. The first year of field education consists of training in evangelism and discipleship, taught by the Nigerian staff of Campus Crusade for Christ. The second year of the field education program entails placement in a local church or other Christian ministry for direct field supervision. To assure that the student has appropriate opportunity for ministry involvement and feedback on his or her ministry activities, a member of the JETS faculty is assigned as co-supervisor. The faculty member assigned to supervise a second year student's field education ministry also functions as that student's faculty advisor.

First, third, and fourth-year students are also assigned faculty advisors. During the second and tenth weeks of each term the chapel periods for the week are given to prayer. During these prayer weeks, students meet in advisee groups with their faculty advisor for sharing and intercession. Faculty members are responsible to create other unstructured opportunities to get to know their advisees and provide counsel regarding academic responsibilities, interpersonal relationships, and ministry skills development.

The JETS faculty includes a full-time chaplain who is an older pastor, highly respected among the ECWA churches. Besides providing pastoral care for all students and systematic discipling for students in the pastoral ministries program, the chaplain serves as pastor of the campus church. In these ways the chaplain provides an on-campus model for students preparing for pastoral ministry.

Parallel to the regular, four-year degree programs, JETS also offers shortened degree programs which are open to graduates of Nigerian three-year post-secondary theological and non-theological institutions. Students admitted to these programs must meet standard JETS admission requirements, plus they must have established a high level of academic performance in their previous training. Students with a diploma from an evangelical seminary are allowed to waive most Bible and theology courses and complete their degree at JETS with two years of specialized studies. Students coming to JETS with secular post-secondary training are required to take a three-year program which includes a full curriculum of Bible and theology courses, plus specialized courses selected to supplement their previous training.

The school operates on a quarter system and runs three quarters per school year. Each quarter consists of ten weeks of class, plus one week of exams. Classes meet for fifty minutes weekly for each unit of credit given. A forty-five-to-ninety-page thesis is required in all degree programs.

In addition to the degree programs offered at JETS, the school also offers two diploma programs designed to meet the training needs of persons called to ministries which do not require degree qualifications. The Diploma in Pastoral Ministries program is similar to the first three years of the degree program in pastoral ministries. The Diploma in Biblical Studies program provides solid training in Bible and theology, plus a special blend of specialized courses to prepare women for teaching and communications ministries. Entrance requirements for the diploma programs are slightly less rigorous than those for the degree programs, and diploma students write comprehensive exams in lieu of a thesis.

Responding to a request from the ECWA leadership, JETS is currently running a pilot program under the provisional designation "Bachelor of Church Ministries." The program intends to address the desire of experienced ECWA pastors who wish to build on previous diploma level studies but lack academic qualification for the Seminary's special degree programs.

The continuing education needs of pastors also are addressed through an "Institute of Pastoral Studies," operated annually during the summer months. The Institute offers experienced pastors three terms of training, leading to a "Certificate in Church Ministries." To ease the burden of pastors who must leave their churches to attend classes on the JETS campus, the curriculum of study is offered in three successive summer terms. To qualify for enrollment in the Institute, a pastor must have accumulated at least ten years of pastoral experience and may not have attended any other institution for formal education within the past five years. The primary language of instruction in the Institute is Hausa.

Finally, JETS offers a special program of Biblical, homemaking, and ministry training for the wives of JETS' diploma and degree students through its "Women's Institute." All married students' wives are required to enroll in the Women's Institute unless they have had a background in theological studies. Women who successfully complete the three-year program of studies are awarded a "Certificate in Bible."

Factors Contributing to the Development of JETS' Approach to Ministry Training

JETS is not the only seminary serving ECWA churches. Igbaja ECWA Theological Seminary was established in 1941 and continues to offer post-secondary training in Bible and theology. In the early 1970s serious discussion about transferring the Igbaja Seminary to a more urban location led to the purchase of a forty-six acre campus on the outskirts of Jos. Further discussion, however, led to a decision to allow Igbaja to retain its original location and to develop a new seminary.

A Curriculum Consultation Committee made up of ECWA educators and church leaders was convened at ECWA Headquarters in Jos during 1979-1980. The Committee indicated that JETS should offer ECWA ministers-in-training an alternative seminary program, not only in location, but also in educational philosophy and curriculum of theological studies.

To provide leadership to the fledgling seminary, veteran missionary and theological educator, Dr. Wilbert Norton, was recruited to serve as the first principal. Closely associated with him from the beginning was Dr. Yusufu Turaki, the Seminary's second principal and currently General Director of the Evangelical Churches of West Africa (ECWA). From the outset, Dr. Norton encouraged Dr. Turaki and his Nigerian colleagues to exercise initiative in laying the curricular and policy foundations for the developing seminary. In response to guidelines established by the ECWA Curriculum Consultation Committee, Dr. Turaki drafted the original JETS curriculum.

Early in 1983, Dr. Victor Cole joined the JETS faculty, and in the same year Dr. Norton resigned his appointment as principal of the Seminary to resume his retirement in the United States. Prior to his departure, however, he assigned Dr. Cole to direct a thorough review and propose revisions of the Seminary's curriculum.

Dr. Cole's approach to that assignment was to involve the faculty in a careful and systematic review of the Seminary's purpose. A philosophy of curriculum development was presented to the faculty in the form of a paper in which Dr. Cole advocated the need to develop an institutional purpose statement, based on a review of the contextual needs of ECWA churches. The resulting purpose statement, then, would constitute the first of five successive steps. In the succeeding steps programs would be derived and justified from the purpose statement, courses would find their rationale in the programs, content would be based on the contribution of each course to the program and institutional goals, and instructional style would be established by the description and purpose of each course.

Utilizing this model, in the summer of 1983 the faculty undertook a study of the JETS curriculum and the needs of ECWA churches. Although several areas of training needs were identified, limited human and material resources forced the faculty to prioritize its energies. The faculty agreed that the Seminary should focus on addressing the church's need for training of pastors, teachers, and communications specialists. It was this decision which led to development of the present three-track degree curriculum.

Other programs at JETS have been developed in direct response to requests for educational services from the constituent church. The diploma programs in Pastoral Ministries and Biblical Studies were initiated in recognition of the inability of some gifted students to attain standards established for entrance to the degree programs. The summer Institute of Pastoral Studies was initiated in 1987 to meet the continuing education needs of ECWA pastors. The Women's Institute, likewise, responds to the request of the ECWA leadership for basic Biblical training for pastors' wives, equipping them to be true partners in ministry. The current pilot program leading to a degree in Church Ministries is another case of the Seminary's attempt to respond to requests received from the constituent church.

It is difficult to isolate specific factors which contributed to development of theological training at JETS. Certainly the historical contribution of Dr. Norton and Dr. Turaki is very significant. Each member of the JETS faculty deserves recognition for contributing toward development of a program which clearly represents a team effort. The Seminary is also fortunate to have a constituent church which is actively interested in theological training and provides open expression of its training needs to the JETS administration. Recent constitution of a JETS Board of Governors, under the able chairmanship of Dr. Chris Abashabi, bodes well for the future development of the Seminary. With respect to the present educational philosophy of the Seminary and the shape of the current curriculum, however, Dr. Victor Cole has exercised considerable influence.

Dr. Cole traces his interest in contextualization of theological education to an undergraduate course on African theologies which he took at Igbaja Theological Seminary. That course, taught by missionary Herbert Klem, piqued the young student's interest in developing evangelical responses to issues raised in the context of African life. A subsequent conversation with Dr. Byang Kato pointed him to papers presented at the first Lausanne Congress on Evangelism, held in 1974, discussing the concept of contextualization.

When this promising young theological student was given the opportunity to continue his education at Dallas Theological Seminary in the U.S.A., he chose as the topic of his 1979 Th.M. thesis, "Contextualization of Theology." Although the topic previously had not been treated at Dallas, Professor Baker was quick and constant in encouraging his student's interest. As he anticipated completion of his Master's program, Cole recognized that contextualization of theology must occur in the context of contextualized theological education. For this reason, his interests turned to curriculum development and led him to enroll at Michigan State University for doctoral studies under the guidance of Professor Ted Ward. It was at M.S.U. that Dr. Cole's interest in educational philosophy and curricularizing strategy was developed. These concepts and commitments have effectively guided the development of the JETS curricula since 1983.

Observations

In reviewing the process of development at JETS, one is struck by the sovereign grace of God by which he prepared in advance those who would be used to provide guidance to this institution. This is most obvious in the case of Dr. Norton, whose missionary service in Africa dates back to the 1930s, but also in the cases of the several Nigerians who have helped to shape the training programs. One missionary's initiative in offering a course on African theologies, at a time when indigenous theologies were suspect among evangelicals, played a pivotal role in the preparation of one who has contributed significantly to the development of the Seminary. Although prepared leadership may be less obvious in other situations than at JETS, it is reassuring to know that the Lord is at work to provide the resources to do his work even before we recognize our needs. It is also encouraging to realize that faithfulness in seemingly insignificant details can be used of God to direct those of his choosing into prepared ministries.

Some will be interested to observe the distribution of courses within the JETS degree curricula. It is common for theological schools to assign the majority of available course hours to Biblical and theological studies, with substantially fewer hours allocated to professional skills development. As the faculty at JETS assessed the needs of the ECWA church, they came to the conviction that more significant professional training was needed.

At that point the faculty adopted an overall curriculum design which concentrates foundational Biblical and theological studies in the first two years of the program, while largely reserving the last two years for professional development. An analysis of course distribution by subject areas indicates that 75 of a total 160 quarter hours of course work can be considered core to the three degree programs (see Table 7.1). This leaves 85 quarter hours available for courses directly related to professional development in the selected field.

TABLE 7.1

Distribution of Core Courses by Subject Area

B.A. in Pastoral Ministries

Christian Life Training	18	11.2 %
Bible Content	21	13.1 %
Bible Study Skills	21	13.1 %
Theo/Philo/History	24	15.0 %
Ministry Skills	44	27.5 %
Research & Thesis	9	5.6 %
African Issues	23	14.4 %
TOTAL	160	

B.A. in Communications Ministries

Christian Life Training	16	10.0 %
Bible Content	18	11.2 %
Bible Study Skills	12	7.5 %
Theo/Philo/History	19	11.9 %
Ministry Skills	73	45.6 %
Research & Thesis	9	5.6 %
African Issues	13	8.1 %
TOTAL	160	

B.A. in Teaching Ministries

Christian Life Training	16	10.0 %
Bible Content	18	11.2 %
Bible Study Skills	12	7.5 %
Theo/Philo/History	16	10.0 %
Ministry Skills	74	46.2 %
Research & Thesis	9	5.6 %
African Issues	15	9.4 %
TOTAL	160	

Core Courses

Christian Life Training	16	10.0 %
Bible Content	18	11.2 %
Bible Study Skills	12	7.5 %
Theology and Ch History	16	10.0 %
African Issues	13	8.1 %
TOTAL CORE	75	46.9 %
PROFESSIONAL	85	53.1 %

This is a much higher ratio of professional to Biblical and theological courses than is found in most theological schools. This has been achieved by providing basic introduction courses, then emphasizing methods of Biblical and theological study. Thus students are equipped to pursue the study of the Scriptures in the context of their future ministries, rather than spending course hours accumulating Biblical and theological content.

Many theological educators will be quick to criticize the curricular strategy adopted by the faculty of JETS, but the ultimate test of any curriculum is the training effect observed in graduates' preparedness for ministry. Scientific outcomes research remains to be done, but *prima facie* evidence indicates that graduates of JETS value their training.[37]

Furthermore, in interviews with an unscientific sample of JETS students, alumni competence in ministry was frequently cited as a positive factor in encouraging interviewees to select JETS as a place of training. This may indicate that the curriculum model employed at JETS deserves more careful consideration.

The approach to contextualization of ministry training at JETS is a second aspect which invites the attention of theological educators. Five courses (totaling 13 quarter hours) comprise the core of contextual studies at JETS, but four additional courses (representing 10 quarter hours) are added in the degree program in Pastoral Ministries (see Table 7.2). Many theological educators, especially those in the Two-Thirds World, will appreciate the diligence of the JETS faculty in focusing contextual issues for theological curricularizing.

Finally, the current experiment with a degree program in Church Ministries raises questions which deserve careful attention of the JETS faculty and Board of Governors. JETS has been cited as an exemplary institution which combines sensitivity to training needs of its constituent church with responsible curricularizing. As the curriculum philosophy adopted by JETS makes clear, care in identifying a program's purpose and justification is appropriate when developing any new course of study. ECWA churches are not alone in desiring theological degrees for their senior pastors. Indeed, this aspiration has been expressed by many churches around the world. When degree aspirants do not possess basic requirements for admission to desired programs, however, theological educators do well to reflect on the motivations underlying these requests.

In some cases mature students without formal credentials are well able to do degree level work. Theological educators will be eased in dealing with such cases by viewing education as a means of personal and professional development. When individuals prove themselves able to fulfill the demands of a program of study, access to learning opportunities should be provided.

Unfortunately, not all who aspire to degrees are prepared to do degree level work, and each case must be judged on its merits. Sometimes requests for special admission to degree programs reflect ignoble motives, and seminaries should beware of requests which hint of an unbiblical preoccupation with status. The New Testament speaks clearly about those who seek to be exalted, and the importance of an attitude of servanthood among the followers of Jesus Christ. Cultural values which run contrary to these Biblical norms should not be encouraged in the church.

This warning also bears significance for theological students and alumni of degree programs. In some cases others view theological degrees as a source of status because seminary graduates employ degrees as instruments of privilege or power. Any theological school which observes such behaviors among its alumni will do well to review its responsibility for cultivating in students those attitudes and values which the Scriptures declare normative for church leadership.

Further Information

Requests for current information about JETS may be addressed to:

Dr. Victor Babajide Cole
Jos ECWA Theological Seminary
Box 5398, Zaria Road
Jos, Plateau State
NIGERIA, West Africa

TABLE 7.2

Courses at JETS Focusing on African Issues

Core Courses

TH 132 Islam—Designed to cover the historical developments, philosophy, theology, and practices concerning the sociopolitical and religious aspects of Islam.

HR 232 Christian Home—Covers the nature of the Christian home, parenting, husband-wife relationship, roles within the home, cultural problems such as extended family responsibilities, relationship with in-laws, and the Biblical injunctions on the parents' role as educators in the home.

HR 411 Sociopolitical African Problems—Designed to introduce the student to political, religious, social, and economic problems facing post-independence African nations. Topics include party politics, political ideologies, ethnicity, coups, and independent church movements.

TH 411 Western and Non-Western Thought—Designed to introduce the student to a comparative analysis of Western and non-Western ideas, mindsets, and worldviews.

HR 431 Man and Culture—Designed to create an awareness of who man is, what culture is, and how culture affects human behaviour. Topics include the origin of culture, its creation, norms, roles, statuses, values, and their influence on social behaviour.

Additional Subjects on African Issues in the Pastoral Ministries Course

HR 231 Church and Society—Covers the relationship of the church and the society including the consequences of this relationship. Topics include social concerns, public awareness, civil rights, inter-faith relationships, and the relationship of the church to civil authorities and politics.

TH 321 Third World Theologies—Covers the development of theological alternatives to the traditional approach to the theology of the Church, against the background of the contextualisation debate in the Third World. Alternatives examined include African theology, Asian theology, and Latin American theology.

TH 421 Islamic Law—Designed to cover the legislation of the Quran, rituals, and ceremonial and social practices. Also covered are family law concerning marriage, divorce, inheritance and adoption, relationships with other faiths, and civil and criminal matters.

TH 422 Comparative Religions—Designed to introduce the student to the philosophy of religions, and the phenomenology and survey of historic and contemporary religions.

CHAPTER 8

Bibelschule Brake
Lemgo, West Germany

Bibelschule Brake (pronounced, BRA-keh) is a three-year Bible institute located in the Federal Republic of Germany which demonstrates flexible strategizing and holistic curricularizing. Much of the energy for development of the institution and its program of training derives from its clearly defined theological commitment and its sensitivity to the context of evangelical churches in Germany.

Description of Ministry Training at Brake

Bibelschule Brake exists for the purpose of training called men and women, equipping them with a knowledge of the Scriptures, and preparing them to participate in the task of world evangelization. This is envisioned as a fourfold responsibility and provides focus for the entire program of ministry training at Brake:

1) to teach the entire Bible
2) to discover and develop students' gifts
3) to further discipleship
4) to prepare for world missions

No Active Recruitment of Students

At Brake, any discussion of ministry training must begin with the process of student selection. Although it is currently the largest Bible school in Germany, Brake does not engage in active recruitment for students. Most students attending the school have come through personal recommendations or by acquaintance with the school through its active evangelistic or summer camp programs.

Prospective students who contact the school are provided with standard application and reference forms. Before an acceptance decision is made, each applicant is personally interviewed by the admissions director. Considerable weight is given to the interview, since the school seeks students who have a spiritual mind and a clear sense of call by God to ministry. Prior academic attainment is accorded less significance (university entrance qualification is not required), since the school has discovered that mature students who are sure of their calling are able to develop academic skills. (The minimum age for application is 18, but the average age of those admitted is 25.) Although many students are very gifted, Brake intends to be a place where ordinary people who are called by God can receive training for ministry.

Distinctive Curriculum Emphasizing Bible and Missions

The curriculum of studies at Brake is distinctive in several respects. Unlike many institutions, Brake offers only one course of study. Within six semesters students receive lectures on all sixty-six books of the Bible. Each semester's schedule of subjects includes lectures on the Old Testament, New Testament, Bible doctrines, practical theology, and missions. Integration of the various subjects into a unified curriculum is provided by the school's overarching commitment to missions training. This is reflected as explicitly in the Bible and theology courses as in those on missions. Through lectures and assignments, the faculty seeks both to develop students' acquaintance with the information of their subjects and to promote self-study skills.

Life and Ministry Training

Although the curriculum of studies is taken seriously by the faculty and staff of Brake, equal priority is assigned to life and ministry training, employing three distinct means.[38]

1) Weekly ministry teams organized by specific ministries. Although participation is required for second- and third-year students, students self-select onto teams, and many students (including some first-year students) serve on more than one team. Ministry teams are student organized and led but supervised by a member of the Brake faculty.

2) Annual evangelistic teams. For one week each year, during the first semester, all students are assigned to evangelistic teams led by members of the Brake faculty. The faculty leader and the ten-to-twelve students making up the team travel together to a community where arrangements have been made in advance to conduct an intensive evangelistic campaign in conjunction with a local church.

3) Program of "practica." Ministry training at Brake is conducted twelve months a year, with eight months given to classroom instruction and four months each year assigned to a practicum.

First-year students routinely serve their practicum on the Brake campus, involved in the school's extensive summer camp program. In the summer camps, practicum assignments may involve direct ministry such as counseling and leading Bible studies for groups of children or very humble service in the kitchen and dorms. Faculty and staff work closely with students during this time, however, observing and correcting both attitudes and procedures.

During the summer following the second and third years of study, students are assisted in locating ministry opportunities in local churches, Christian organizations, or foreign missions. Each practicum situation must include a specific job description and be approved by the Brake faculty. Students are required to do their practica in different types of ministries and are not allowed to do a practicum in their home church during their first or second year. In each practicum situation the supervising pastor or missionary is required to provide personal oversight of the student, meeting daily with the student for prayer and direction in ministry.

At the conclusion of each practicum the supervisor is required to complete a narrative evaluation of the student and her or his ministry performance and review that evaluation with the student. Upon return to campus, the evaluation is reviewed again with the student by a member of the Brake faculty, and specific plans are developed to address any areas of weakness in character or ministry skills which became evident in the course of the practicum. An unsatisfactory practicum report may be cause for dismissal from the Bible college. The value and priority of the practica at Brake is attested by allocation of one-third of each student's period of enrollment to this activity.

Life Training

In addition to academic instruction and ministry training, the faculty of Brake also are committed to life training for their students. Primary responsibility in this regard is shared by the "class teacher," the student deans, and the faculty and staff at large.

One member of the faculty is assigned as "class teacher" to each entering class and normally retains that appointment throughout the three years of that class's enrollment. During that time the class teacher is responsible to develop a personal relationship with members of the class which provides freedom to counsel and advise. Often official communication with students is channeled through their class teacher.

Brake also has student deans who are active in counseling students. Counseling may be initiated by the student or, when areas of weakness become evident in life interactions, by the deans.

As part of its program of life training, Brake assigns students to eight hours per week of manual labor under the supervision of various members of the campus staff. Through extensive contact with students over an extended period of time, staff have opportunities to observe students' character development, often in unguarded moments. The principal meets weekly with staff supervisors for coordination and focus, and staff view the student work program as an important opportunity for input into the spiritual development of students.

In addition to formal contacts in class and ministry, Brake faculty also enjoy numerous informal occasions to develop relationships with students. Most faculty specifically announce their availability to students, and some routinely invite groups of students for times of social interaction and fellowship in their homes.

The various components of Brake's program of life training converge each year when the full faculty and staff meet to discuss character evaluations for all students. Each student is evaluated across six character qualities.[39] In preparation for the character review session, the class teacher drafts an evaluation of each student in his or her class.

This statement is presented to the full faculty and staff and is open for discussion and revision. Since various members of the faculty and staff routinely see students in different relationships, care is taken to develop a character evaluation which represents all perspectives. In any case where serious character weaknesses are noted, one member of the faculty or staff is assigned to counsel with the student regarding his or her problem. When these efforts are not successful, students may be requested to withdraw from school temporarily or permanently. This reflects the school's conviction that an effective minister must do the truth as well as know it.

Summer Camps

No description of Bibelschule Brake's response to the training needs of the evangelical church in Germany would be complete without including the school's extensive program of summer camps. Five two-week camp programs are offered each year,[40] with an emphasis on spiritual nurture and family recreation.[41] Brake's family camp program is intergenerational by design, with special programs provided for school age children, and babysitting or planned activities available for infants and preschool children.

The school's beautiful campus setting has been thoughtfully developed for this use and includes a park area with duck pond, an extensive sand play area, an 18-hole mini-golf course, volleyball courts, and a soccer field. Bible teaching sessions and inspirational messages are provided by members of the Brake faculty, so that campers have an opportunity to grow spiritually under the instructional and ministry gifts of the Bible school faculty.

Practicum students, who serve as staff to the camps, minister in the children's programs, provide support services, and have opportunity to observe their teachers in ministry. The period before the camping season begins is used for site preparation and staff training, and to allow students two weeks of personal vacation time. Brake's summer camp program has met with overwhelming acceptance by evangelical Christians throughout Germany, Switzerland, and Austria. Although publicity is minimal, most camps are booked to capacity (220 campers) well in advance.

Faculty modeling is a recurrent theme recognizable in several of the programs described above. This is not accidental but reflects a basic conviction about the nature of ministry training at Brake. As one member of the faculty expressed it, "Life begets life." It is as faculty have opportunity to share their lives with students, and students have opportunity to observe the outflow of faculty lives in ministry, that student lives are formed.

Factors Contributing to the Development of Brake's Approach to Ministry Training

Bibelschule Brake was founded in 1959 as the result of another school's decision to eliminate training for missionary service from its curriculum. At that time, three members of the other school's staff (including its founder) were convinced of a great need among German churches for evangelical missionary training. When this conviction was supported by the urgent request from German students, the decision was made to open a new school, now known as Bibelschule Brake. Thus, from its very inception, Brake has existed in response to needs existing in the evangelical churches of Germany.

From the outset Brake has been designed as a missions training program. As missionaries and pastors themselves, the founders knew that missionary training must be life oriented. This led to developing the extensive program of life and ministry training in effect today. They also believed that motivation to mission arises out of an understanding of God's heart for the lost world. They were convinced that knowledge of the Scriptures provides both the stimulus and the message of missions. In an era when neo-orthodoxy seemed to be carrying the day in Europe, Brake developed a curriculum of studies based on allegiance to an inerrant Scripture. The curriculum of teaching the whole Bible which was developed at that time and continues today reflects this confidence in the centrality and trustworthiness of the Scriptures.

All three men who were instrumental in founding Brake continued active in the Bible school for nearly two decades, and throughout that time the same man served as principal. When he left the school in 1978 to take up another ministry, the present principal, Rev. Doyle Klaassen, was appointed. Although another of the three founders has since left the school, one continues to carry a full teaching load and serve as a valued member of the staff. This continuity of influence and leadership has provided invaluable stability of vision and purpose within the Bible school. The story of Brake is not one of reassessment and change, but rather one of prayerfully holding to the principles on which the school was founded.

Observations

The last point is significant. Continuity of leadership and purpose is of great advantage to a ministry training program. This observation may seem out of place in a study of renewal of theological education, but responsible renewal is never promoted as change for the sake of change. When institutional purpose and philosophy are biblically founded and oriented to the specific training needs of the constituent church, change is unnecessary and ill advised. Not all schools, however, enjoy this heritage. Furthermore, occasional long-term shifts in the ministry training needs of the constituent church demand new or modified responses from theological training institutions. Openness to change in such situations, combined with a stability of theological and institutional focus, is the challenge which faces all theological educators.

Brake represents an institution which has been able to step outside its normal role of training professional ministers and missionaries to provide significant lay training for evangelical Christians in German-speaking Europe. By packaging the program as summer camps, Christians are enabled to combine spiritual nurture and family recreation during their holidays. In a context where many evangelical believers do not attend congregations which provide sound Biblical instruction, this is a significant ministry.

There is a corollary danger, however, for believers from evangelical congregations. If the spiritual blessings received at Brake have the effect of encouraging believers to look to the Bible college instructors, rather than their own pastors, for Christian nurture, the congregation and the Church of Jesus Christ is weakened. Although this danger is minimized by the relative brevity of each camper's presence at Brake, schools considering more extensive lay training programs need to beware of potential negative effects. The most effective insurance against this danger is active recruitment of respected pastors and church leaders into advisory roles, and careful attentiveness to the concerns they voice and the advice they provide.

Perhaps the most challenging aspect of Brake's approach to missionary training is its extensive provision for developing the spiritual life and ministry skills of students. Some aspects of the Bible school's program are easily transferable and already have been adopted by other Bible schools in Germany.

Theological schools which currently give primary attention in student selection to previous academic performance would do well to consider Brake's focus on spiritual maturity. This is especially crucial in areas where public education channels students into vocational streams based on early testing programs. Other schools may find that maturity, a heart for God, and a clear sense of call to ministry more than offset early educational deficiencies. On educational criteria, the twelve men Jesus chose were very ordinary. This observation may have more significance for student selection by ministry training programs than is commonly recognized today.

Ministry training at Brake through weekly ministry teams, annual evangelistic teams, and summer practica is a model which invites reflection at several points. Many schools have incorporated a period of "internship" into their training curricula, but few have pursued the logic of training in the context of ministry as far as Brake.

The school supports its requirement of three to four months in ministry by noting that development of character and ministry skills requires time. Four-week, or even six-week, hit-and-run forays cannot produce the same training effect. By requiring practica in all three years of the training program, furthermore, students obtain a variety of experiences, and the developmental effect is multiplied. In situations where so extensive a program of practica is not feasible, theological educators need to assess the deficiencies created in their programs and seek creative means to provide significant ministry training.

Two aspects of Brake's program of life training merit comment. Some schools which require students to work on campus have yet to organize these programs for character development. At Brake, the principal's constant encouragement to staff supervisors is an important factor in preserving this focus.

The program of annual character evaluation of each student by the full faculty and staff is justified by two convictions: a good character is essential to effective Christian ministry, and all members of the faculty and staff can make valuable contributions to development of effective ministers. This, of course, bears heavy implications for selection of staff, as well as faculty. Where these convictions are shared, however, others may be attracted to a similar procedure.

Finally, those who concur that "life begets life" will be challenged by the willingness of Brake faculty to submit themselves as models for their students. There is an unhealthy form of modeling which draws attention to oneself and one's gifts. This is completely foreign to the context at Brake. There faculty share their own heart for the Lord and actively engage in ministry, while urging students to look beyond themselves to the Lord as the only fully adequate model. Not all schools will be prepared to choose this route. Faculty which reject this role in favor of scholastic or rationalizing models, however, will do well to examine the spirituality and effectiveness produced in their students.

Further Information

Requests for current information about Brake may be addressed to:

Herr Doyle Klaassen, Schulleiter
Bibelschule Brake
Postfach 3040
D-4920 Lemgo 1, West Germany

Telephone: (49) 5261-8090

Chapter 9

All Nations Christian College
Easneye, Ware, Hertfordshire, U.K.

All Nations Christian College (ANCC) is a British, university level, interdenominational missionary training college which demonstrates spiritual formation, holistic curricularizing, and a developmental focus. The entire program of the college reflects a creative adaptation of traditional training patterns for the specific purpose of preparing students for effective missionary service.

Description of Missionary Training at ANCC

Although a minority of students come to ANCC for one year or less, the basic training program of the college is two years in length, consisting of three, ten-week terms per year. Upon admission, each student is assigned a tutor who accepts responsibility for the spiritual, academic, and ministry development of the student during the following school year.[42]

The college offers a schedule of lecture subjects, identified as "core subjects" and "elective subjects," in which the staff of the college addresses various topics of importance in missionary life and ministry.[43] All students normally are required to attend lectures and do assignments for all thirty-four core subjects. Students may be required to do specific "elective" subjects as well. The typical subject consists of ten hours of lecture, plus at least fifteen hours of private study by the student (although the lecture time may vary from as few as five hours to as many as twenty). It is the responsibility of each lecturer to develop assignments for his or her subject. Nevertheless, assignments for all subjects are made individually by each student's tutor and are submitted to the tutor. The typical assignment calls for a 3000-4000 word paper exploring some facet of the topic discussed in lectures, often in a way that has specific significance for the life and ministry of the student.[44]

Because of its distinct focus on cross-cultural missionary training, ANCC only accepts students who have a clear sense of God's call to cross-cultural ministry. The conditions of entry favor mature students (minimum age is 23), who have completed some course of post-high school study and have experience in an occupation and in their local church. Prospective applicants are advised to consult with their church leaders before application so that the church can be involved in planning and recommendations for their missionary career. Since married couples serve together on the mission field, both husband and wife must apply and be accepted as students at ANCC. (In order to facilitate this arrangement, the college operates a licensed nursery to care for pre-school children during morning lecture hours.) Many students who attend the college already have cross-cultural ministry experience.

Because missionaries are often called upon to speak to large and small groups, the college provides specific training in communication skills. In addition to lectures and demonstrations, students are organized into speakers' groups for simulated speaking opportunities. Sermons, Bible lessons, talks to student and youth groups, and interviews by mission boards or councils are all covered in the speakers' groups.

In order to provide practical application of training, the College's Department of Christian Ministries works closely with area churches and organizations to assign students to weekend and block placement ministries. Weekend ministry assignments are made by ministry teams.

At the beginning of each school year, ministry team assignments seek to match experienced and entering students with local church ministry opportunities according to the needs of the congregation and the gifts of the students. Since the ministry team assignment is viewed as an important part of the student's training as well as an opportunity for service, the supervising pastor or minister is requested to meet with the team at least once each term for prayer, discussion of ministry performance, direction regarding areas for improvement, and planning for the future. In addition to feedback given to the student, a member of the ANCC staff visits the church as necessary to receive reports from the supervising pastor or minister and to assist with areas which may require extra attention.

Each term some students' ministry team assignment is to a "speakers pool" or to the "Easneye Bible School," rather than to a local church. Those in the speakers pool are available to accept invitations received by the college for speakers in churches, student Christian Unions, schools, and hospitals. Easneye Bible School is a Saturday institute which is organized and operated by students of the College for Christian laymen and women in Ware and its vicinity. Under the supervision of the College staff, students assigned to Easneye Bible School receive practical experience for missionary school and lay training ministries. Testimony to the effectiveness of this program is the encouraging reception and support the Bible school receives from Christians in the community.

Students are also given opportunity to apply training through a block ministry placement, normally scheduled during the second term of the second year. At this time students are assigned to a church or Christian organization for a five-to-eight-week period of full-time ministry involvement. The block placement intends to provide opportunity for students to work directly under experienced Christian leaders and observe their own strengths and weaknesses in an authentic ministry situation.

Students are expected to be meaningfully involved in ministry from the beginning of the placement. In church placements, the supervising pastor is requested to meet daily with the student for prayer and briefing and to provide appropriate assignments and direction for ministry. In organizational placements, this responsibility is assumed by the student's ministry supervisor. The supervisor or pastor is also requested to submit to the Department of Christian Ministries a confidential report on the student's preparedness and performance in ministry at the conclusion of the placement.

Since several students are able to arrange overseas placements which satisfy the requirements of the College, this also can be a significant time of testing one's missionary call in a cross-cultural situation. Upon return from the block placement, students are assigned to debriefing groups where they have opportunity to reflect with tutors and peers on their experience in the block ministry placement and on the lessons learned through it.

Academic and spiritual training at ANCC is complemented with practical training in skills many missionaries find necessary. The practical studies program includes both "full courses" and "short courses." Full courses are offered one afternoon per week for a term or half-term, while short courses are one day (or half a day) in length, typically offered on a Saturday. Full practical courses include car maintenance (elementary and advanced), food production, first aid, home nursing and tropical hygiene, and building. Short courses offer instruction in photography (elementary and advanced), bookshop practice, basic cookery, hairdressing, and dentistry (specifically, procedures for emergency extractions). Students are expected to enroll in at least one full course and one short course each term, although most exceed that level. Participation of students in practical courses, as in every other aspect of life and training at ANCC, is discussed with the student's tutor.

Although ANCC is a college, it functions very much as a community. Beyond the learning, worship, and social dimensions of the community life, staff and students of the College work together as well. Daily chores and maintenance responsibilities are assigned, not only as a means of reducing operating costs, but also as an opportunity to develop and demonstrate teamwork and faithfulness in service. Teamwork, encouragement, and helping skills are also developed through sporting activities scheduled each Wednesday afternoon.

Tutors at ANCC have considerable input into the lives of their students. Three times weekly tutors meet with their students for small group worship. Although ministry team assignments are coordinated by the College's Department of Christian Ministry, students regularly discuss experiences in ministry with their own tutor. In addition, tutors are encouraged to take their lunch with students, join in daily student coffee parties, and schedule evening social gatherings for their tutorial group as occasions to get to know students better. The tutor, therefore, is responsible to weave the various aspects of the college program into an integrated—and individualized—curriculum for each student's personal and professional development. It is this highly personalized, intensely developmental context for missionary preparation which distinguishes ANCC and constitutes it a model of ministry training that other theological educators may want carefully to consider.

Factors Contributing to the Development of ANCC's Approach to Ministry Training

The history of All Nations Christian College finds its origins in the founding of All Nations Missionary Union in 1892 even though a college was not begun until 1923. The present program of missionary training owes its design to innovations introduced following the appointment of a new principal in 1961.

Michael David Morris was a former missionary to Nigeria who came to the College when he was prevented from returning to Africa by the ill health of his child. As a missionary, Morris had been committed to building relationships with Nigerians which made the gospel relevant to that society. In his new position as principal, the same commitment to relevant missionary ministry guided his leadership.

Since the enrollment of the College stood at only fifteen, Morris recognized the need and opportunity for change. Despite considerable resistance from an instinctively conservative board, Morris sharpened the College's focus on missionary preparation, revised the syllabus, and determined to build a new kind of college staff. The staff Morris envisioned should combine four qualities—they must come to the college with successful missionary experience, they must be able communicators and teachers, they must have demonstrated pastoral gifts, and they must possess a team spirit, each willing to blend unique gifts and contributions toward the common goal of preparing students for relevant missionary ministries.

Being aware that single men and women work together on the mission field, along with missionary couples, Morris reasoned they should also be prepared together. In 1971, All Nations Bible College shed its reputation as a school for men, merged with two women's missionary training colleges, and adopted its current name. Under Morris's leadership, the new college continued to develop the program of holistic development for missionary service which is the hallmark of the institution today. It is testimony to Morris's wisdom that the principles he established continue to guide the College today.

At ANCC, therefore, change came as the result of one man's vision, creativity, and tenacity. It was a vision, however, which was born out of field experience, creativity which was willing to rethink training strategies on the basis of desired outcomes, and tenacity which was willing to work for renewal of ministry training despite protestations that "we have not done it that way before." Patience was important, too, for it allowed him to wait for God to bring to the College staff members who would share these commitments and be able to implement them in life and training.

Observations

All Nations Christian College is unique in many ways, and other theological educators may be tempted to focus on that uniqueness. Two observations may be offered regarding the process of program renewal at ANCC, however. Furthermore, several aspects of the current program may have more transferability than appear on the surface.

It was noted above that the opportunity to introduce change at ANCC in 1961 was facilitated by the smallness of the college at that time. One might well wonder if change of similar magnitude could successfully be introduced today at ANCC—or in another school, for that matter—with a roster of nearly 200 students and 16 academic staff. There is an inertia inherent in largeness which is resistant to change.

This does not exempt larger schools from the quest for renewal of theological education, but it does point to two things: First, larger schools will have to work harder to realize renewal, and persons associated with those schools must accept the burden of paying this higher price. Second, implementation of the most creative and thoroughgoing changes will likely arise first in the smaller theological schools. This warns theological educators against the natural tendency to focus on the larger and better known schools as models for ministry training. They should accept, as well, the challenge of discovering those smaller institutions around the world where training experiments and innovations are being pioneered.

A second observation relates to the role of one man—a principal—in effecting significant change at ANCC. It is totally incredible that ANCC should have become the institution it is today if God had not raised up Mr. Morris. It is even more difficult to believe that major change could successfully have been implemented if he, as principal, had opposed it.

This points up the determinative role of institutional leadership in the change process. When major change is needed, commitment must exist at a leadership level; bottom up radical change is almost impossible. This stands as a great challenge to those who bear institutional leadership responsibilities. At the same time, it constitutes a warning to those who desire renewal of theological education in their institution but are faced with opposition from the school's highest administrators. Faculty in that situation will be wise to attempt to win their administrators to the cause of renewal; board members may be forced to consider administrative reappointments. Administrators, faculty, and board members alike will do well to bear in mind that "unless the Lord builds a house, they labor in vain who build it." Renewal of theological education demands much prayer.

Beyond these general observations, several elements of the ANCC approach to training may be transferable to other ministry training programs.

1) Highly defined focus—The highly defined focus of training at ANCC clearly has had a beneficial effect on development of the College's program. Other institutions may find similar advantage in reexamining and sharpening their training objective.

2) Successful practitioners as trainers—Trainers reproduce themselves. Institutions which affirm they exist to train practitioners may find it helpful, therefore, to reexamine the criteria used to select faculty and staff.

3) Holistic development of students for ministry—If a faculty is agreed that an effective minister combines personal, spiritual, informational, and practical qualities, they will do well to determine if each of those areas is appropriately represented in their training curricula.

Addressing the issue of holistic development for ministry is one thing; assuring that it occurs is another. Other schools may boggle at the thought of making one staff person uniquely responsible for monitoring and guiding each student's development, but the strategy clearly benefits students at ANCC. If holistic development is important, then strategies (and structures?) should be implemented to assure that it occurs. Those who reject ANCC's approach clearly bear a responsibility to develop an alternative.

4) Resisting the temptation to compromise purpose for growth—By British standards, ANCC is not a small Bible college.[45] On the other hand, ANCC annually receives 1000 applications for the 100 places open in each entering class. Very few educational institutions in the world enjoy that level of competition for entrance. It would be easy to conclude that the college should be allowed to grow from 200 to 500, and perhaps later to 800. To do so, however, would incur irreversible changes in the life of the College as a community and in the nature of staff to student relationships. ANCC is unwilling to accept those consequences for the sake of growth.

This appears to reflect great wisdom, since the compromises required would threaten the very qualities which distinguish the College as a desirable place for missionary training. In an era when budgets are tight and largeness seems to assure fiscal stability, other school administrators may want to consider ANCC's response to the issues of institutional purpose and growth.

Further Information

Requests for current information about ANCC may be addressed to:

Rev. C. David Harley, Principal
All Nations Christian College
Easneye, Ware
Hertfordshire SG12 8LX England

Telephone: (0920) 61243

CHAPTER 10

Union Biblical Seminary
Pune, Maharashtra State, India

Union Biblical Seminary (UBS) is an Asian residential seminary offering ministry training at the graduate and undergraduate levels. The seminary demonstrates holistic curricularizing and developmental focus, as well as several other renewal values, in a creative restructuring of training for ministry.

Description of Ministry Training at UBS

Admission to UBS each year is granted to approximately 15 pre-theology students, 25 B.Th. students, and 50 B.D. students from a pool of applicants two to three times that number. Selection is based on previous academic achievement, evidence of call and experience in ministry, recommendations of the applicant's church and Christian leaders, and successful performance on entrance examinations. The Seminary also offers training at the Master of Theology (M.Th.) level to qualified candidates.

New students are required to report to the UBS campus in Pune during the first week of June for a six-week "Orientation Session." During this term the focus is on identifying student strengths and weaknesses and on introducing students to theological study. An intensive course on English (written and oral) and study skills focuses on developing disciplines needed for understanding and analysis. Carefully designed field trips to sites of cultural and religious interest in the Pune area are followed by guided exercises to develop skills of observation and reflection. The presence of third-year students on campus during the same period allows the first-year students to observe their seniors in reflection and dialogue. During the orientation session, students also receive a basic introduction to Biblical languages and begin study of principles of leadership in the local church.

The regular school year begins in mid-July and proceeds on a semester schedule to mid-March.[46] During the first year, emphasis is placed on developing sound methods of Bible study (including the study of at least one Biblical language through the intermediate level) and cultivating ministry gifts and skills.

At the end of the first academic year, each student is required to enter a thirteen-and-a-half month internship assignment, beginning immediately upon the close of the first-year classes and continuing to the first week of June in the following year.[47] The place of internship may be provided by the student's sponsoring church or parachurch organization or may be arranged by the UBS Internship Department. Each intern is assigned a supervisor, who must agree to meet with the intern at least biweekly to review ministry plans and progress and to provide nurture and counsel.

Each intern is also assigned a tutor (who may or may not be the supervisor) to direct his or her studies during the internship year. Because the internship is intended to cultivate positive habits for ongoing study and ministry, students are required to complete four courses (approximately one semester's work) while in internship. Courses prescribed during the internship are provided with carefully designed, interactive study guides. An introductory session, prior to leaving campus, orients students to the courses to be studied. Regular assignments are given for discussion with the tutor and submission to the UBS teaching staff. These courses are also designed to take maximum advantage of the student's location in context by requiring collection of field data or interviews with persons in the community, avoiding a single-eyed focus on text and library materials.

Students, supervisors, and tutors are provided with forms and a schedule for reporting to the Internship Coordinator at the UBS campus. In addition, each student is visited on site at least once during the year by the Internship Coordinator, and twice during the year by different members of the UBS teaching staff. Students also return to the UBS campus twice during the internship year, once for college exams in October, and a second time for Senate of Serampore exams in March and April.

Students return to campus the first week of June, following the internship year, for a "Reflection Session" which coincides with the "Orientation Session" of incoming students. During the reflection session, each student shares a report of his or her internship experience and benefits from the insights and comments of peers and faculty. Various case studies,[48] prepared during the internship describing situations experienced or observed, are also presented to the group for reflection and interaction. Since some sessions are open to first-year students, they gain the opportunity to learn from the experience and reflective example of their seniors.

The third academic year commences in mid-July and continues through mid-March of the following year. Courses during the third year are designed to capitalize on the student's experience in ministry and to refine skills of Biblical study and theological reflection. In March, graduating students write their final examinations and, if successful, receive their degrees.

Although this combination of on-campus and off-campus study directly facilitates integration of learning and practice, the UBS staff provides other structures for nurturing Christian character and values and developing ministry skills. This is done through practical training teams, "Ministry Today" groups, chapel services, and community life activities.

Practical Training Teams

During the first and third years, each student is assigned to a practical training team. Teams may consist of two to ten students who are involved in weekend ministry at one local church or outreach area. Each ministry team is assigned a faculty advisor, who is responsible to assure that each member of the team receives meaningful opportunities for ministry and is faithful in fulfilling that ministry. Ministry teams meet biweekly, during the designated hour on Monday, for planning and prayer. On alternate weeks, the entire seminary family gathers for reports from practical training teams and a time of corporate worship and prayer.

"Ministry Today" Groups

Pastoral care of students at UBS is provided through "Ministry Today" groups. A Ministry Today group consists of ten to twelve students, constituted to provide a mixture of classes, denominational backgrounds, and regional and language groups. Each Ministry Today group is assigned a staff advisor and selects its own student leader.

Time is allotted in the Seminary schedule for Ministry Today groups to meet twice weekly. Wednesday discussion sessions are slotted for one-and-a-half hours, while Thursday worship times are set for thirty minutes only. An advisory committee, made up of Seminary administrators, assigns topics and provides materials for the discussion sessions and selects passages for worship times. The student leader is responsible to assure that each member of the Ministry Today group is given equal opportunity to lead discussion and worship sessions.

Topics covered in the discussion sessions may include the campus guide of conduct, a technical paper on liberation theology, or practical aspects of missions and ethics. Ministry Today groups also take an active part in preparation for the Seminary's annual "Days of Challenge" camp for youth with pre-camp sessions given to one-on-one witnessing, counseling techniques, and prayer preparation for campers and the camp program.

Members of the UBS staff attach high priority to their role as Ministry Today group advisors, regularly attending scheduled meetings and building relationships with individual students. In the course of the school year, the staff advisor schedules six appointments with each member of his or her Ministry Today group to gain a more personal understanding of the students and the particular challenges they face. Three hours are reserved in the weekly schedule for student interviews with Ministry Today group advisors. Besides these structured times, staff advisors often invite members of their Ministry Today group to their home or arrange to meet together off campus. The Seminary recognizes the importance of these advisor-student relationships by including a student's Ministry Today group advisor in any administrative or academic discussion relating to the student.

Although the Ministry Today groups are deliberately structured to bring together students from widely varying backgrounds, a warm sense of identity tends to develop among members of each group. Emergencies faced by one member are viewed as crises for all, and all pitch in to assist the one in need. Thus, besides providing a context for faculty advisement, the Ministry Today groups encourage and cultivate mutual caring among students—and that across cultural and denominational lines.

Community Life Activities

UBS also provides on-campus housing for single and married students, and conducts an active program of campus sports and community activities coordinated by the Union Biblical Seminary Student Association (UBSSA). The work of UBSSA is structured under student committees which organize and direct prayer vigils, missionary involvement, social and cultural programs, literary publications, service ministries, and handicraft projects. An annual sports day affords opportunity for keen competition, but campus facilities for basketball, football, volleyball, cricket, and ping-pong invite frequent recreation.

Three times a week the UBS community gathers for chapel. On Tuesday and Friday the staff and students gather for devotions, but on Wednesday afternoon the community gathers for corporate worship.

Self-Evaluation Exercise

Twice each school year each student is requested to complete a personal self-evaluation exercise which touches on every aspect of life and leadership skills. Similar evaluation reports are prepared by a fellow student (usually a roommate) and the student's Ministry Today advisor. These reports are forwarded to the Ministry Today advisor who collates the reports and discusses a summary report with the student. The summary report, as well as individual reports, are forwarded to the Dean of Students, who presents a report on each student to the Seminary staff. Semiannual staff evaluation of all students requires a major investment of staff time which is justified by the Seminary's commitment to promote growth and development in the lives of students.

Extension Education

Besides its campus programs, UBS also has a significant and highly regarded program of extension education. Extension education at UBS has taken a different course than many TEE programs around the world. The majority of students (155 active in 1989) are enrolled in the English language B.D. program which, like UBS's campus B.D., is recognized by the Senate of Serampore College. (Smaller Hindi and Marathi language programs at the B.Th. level are also offered.)

Students enrolling in the extension department are assigned a tutor by the Seminary. A tutor must have B.D. qualifications himself and must reside in close enough proximity to the student to make possible monthly visits. The student is provided with self-instructional texts and a list of assignments. On a schedule set by the Seminary, the student is to meet with his or her tutor for discussion of the lessons completed and the assignments done. Certain assignments, furthermore, are designated for submission to the Seminary for grading. Four times in the course of their extension study program, students are required to attend two-week seminars on the UBS campus. This provides opportunity for students to experience campus life, interact with the instructors who wrote their study materials, and make use of the Seminary's library.

The study guides developed for use in the UBS B.D. program were written by the lecturers who teach those subjects on campus. The study guides do not employ formal programming methods often associated with TEE but are designed to direct the student's personal study of the subject matter. Students are given reading assignments in standard textbooks, required to collect data from their community or congregation, or assigned Bible passages for study and exposition. The study guide provides questions for review and reflection on the materials

studied and often suggests appropriate responses to the questions
posed. The study guides frequently supplement text materials with
additional information which campus students may receive through
class lectures. Finally, the study guides provide assignments to be
discussed with the tutor or to be submitted to the Seminary.

The Seminary also operates a busy program of continuing education seminars for pastors and Christian workers. During 1987-88, three
hundred pastors and lay leaders participated in six workshops offered
by the UBS staff. This program is expected soon to receive a major boost
with completion of a large continuing education center now under
construction. The continuing education center will provide accomoda-
tion and dining facilities for groups up to seventy, enabling the Seminary to more effectively strengthen the ministries of Christian workers
throughout west-central India.

Factors Contributing to the Development of UBS's Approach to Ministry Training

UBS has not always operated on its present program of ministry
training. In fact, the program described above has only been in place for
two years. The Seminary was founded in 1953, through efforts initiated
by the newly formed Evangelical Fellowship of India, in response to the
widely felt need for a graduate level theological college to serve the
evangelical church of India. Initially the Seminary occupied the campus
of the Free Methodist Biblical Training School in Yeotmal (more recently
know as Yavatmal), in central Maharashtra State. Almost immediately
the new seminary became a center of training for evangelical ministers
from every state in India, as well as other nations of South Asia. Over
the next twenty years emphasis was placed on strengthening the instructional programs of the Seminary and developing an Indian faculty.
The approach to ministry training during this period followed patterns
familiar to theological educators in the West.

The growth and interregional composition of the student body
placed increasing stress on the need to provide students with meaningful Christian ministry opportunities. Since Yeotmal is not a large city
and is located in an exclusively Marathi-speaking area, opportunities in
that locale were limited. In 1971 a decision was taken by the Executive
Committee of the UBS Board of Governors to "investigate the possibility of relocating Union Biblical Seminary in a strategically located
cosmopolitan city."[49] In 1975 the Board of Governors voted unani-
mously to transfer the Seminary to Pune.[50]

The proposed relocation was effected in 1983 and opened opportunities for ministry and outreach beyond the grandest expectations of the

Seminary staff. The Practical Training Department of the Seminary can now place all 225 students in meaningful ministry assignments with ample scope for additional ministries. During this period, however, the staff began to recognize that weekend involvement was not providing the Seminary's graduates with adequate preparation for on-going ministry.

From the introduction of theological education by extension (TEE) into India in 1971, UBS was an active member of The Association For Theological Education by Extension (TAFTEE). Over the intervening years TAFTEE's efforts have focused on bachelor and certificate levels and have adhered to a classical TEE format employing programmed instructional materials and weekly tutorial sessions.

By 1978, UBS determined to launch an off-campus program that would extend its Serampore-affiliated B.D. to students who were unable to leave their ministry locations. In recognition of the more extensive educational background and widely dispersed settings of potential B.D. extension students, the Seminary opted for an approach which allowed for independent study and substituted periodic interaction with a UBS-appointed tutor for the weekly seminars usually associated with TEE. UBS is fortunate that the original Director of Extension Studies was Robin Thomson, a creative and energetic Englishman, who was born to missionary parents in India and had spent most of his life in that country. Under Thomson's leadership the whole UBS instructional staff was involved in production of self-study materials for the extension program.

The UBS extension B.D. program enrolled its first students in 1981. As enrollment began to grow, the staff of the Seminary could not avoid noting that papers submitted by extension students routinely reflected a level of academic-ministry integration which was painfully absent from most papers submitted on campus. As tutors reported on the progress of extension students and members of the Seminary staff had occasion to visit extension students in their place of ministry, another factor became evident. Whereas campus students tended to view study as a task to be undertaken prior to ministry, extension students recognized study as a discipline integral to ministry.

Even before campus relocation and launching of the TEE program, the Board of Governors was aware of a need for more effective training. In 1979 it appointed a "curriculum revision commission," convened by Narendra John, a member of the staff with doctoral training in curriculum development. Two major results were realized during the two years of this project. First, the staff clarified their training goals in a document titled, "Servant-Leaders for the Church in India."[51] These goals were then spelled out in objectives for different courses and activities of the seminary. This shifted the emphasis of the curriculum from covering prescribed content to attaining training goals. The second major product of the commission was the program of "Ministry Today" groups described above.

By 1982, various members of the UBS staff felt a keen desire for a more objective appraisal of the effectiveness of training provided by the Seminary. In that year the administration approached a mature and gifted senior student with the proposal that he study the UBS alumni's view of the adequacy of their training.[52] The time available was not adequate to pursue a thorough study, and the response rate of alumni to the questionnaire sent out was a disappointing 20%.

Nevertheless, the findings seemed significant. Alumni provided strongly positive assessments of their experiences in chapel, weekend ministries, and extra-curricular activities during training. Only 60% of respondents, however, reported that classroom instruction at UBS was relevant and helpful to them in their ministries. Fully 30%, on the other hand, reported that instruction was irrelevant. Respondents also indicated that extensive use of the lecture method contributed to an impersonal air in the classroom and precluded meaningful interaction between teachers and students. Furthermore, even the 60% which gave a positive assessment of their training expressed a self-confidence which the researcher found alarming. He warned:

> If the alumni will go out from the Seminary depending totally upon the content they had lernt in the classrooms, the content might not be adequate to meet the need of the people. They must go out with a deep sense of dependence upon the Lord who is the source of all wisdom and knowledge. The alumni should have a clear understanding that Christ is the only adequate source for the need of the people. The training programme should help the alumni to realize his or her inadequacy.[53]

In January 1984, Australian educationist Dr. Brian Hill visited the UBS campus and presented to the instructional staff a paper titled, "Theological Education: Is It Out of Practice?"[54] The paper struck a responsive chord among the staff and sparked considerable discussion. Two years passed, however, before the specific issues raised by Hill were to take the shape of a specific proposal for curriculum change.

In keeping with the Seminary's commitment to serve the church, a consultation with leaders of sponsoring churches and organizations was convened in March 1985. As the Seminary staff explored with church leaders the effectiveness of graduates in ministry, two facts came to light. First, UBS graduates were recognized as highly knowledgeable and able expositors of the Scriptures. On the other hand, however, alumni of the Seminary generally were weak in relational and pastoral skills required for effective ministry.

In the spring of 1986, Robin Thomson drafted a paper titled, "How to Strengthen Our Training: A Proposal for Integrating Supervised Field Experience (Ministry and Study) Into Our Curriculum."[55] Together with an article by TAFTEE staff members Vinay Samuel and Chris Sugden titled, "Theological Education for the Mission of the Church in India,"[56] Thomson's paper was circulated to members of the UBS instructional staff for discussion at the pre-session faculty retreat. In his paper, Thomson proposed stretching the B.D. to a four-year program of study, with the second and third years spent in a combined ministry-study internship placement. Since materials and systems to support study in context already existed in the Seminary's extension department, the principal unanswered questions related to the wisdom of so radical a reconfiguration of the traditional B.D. curriculum, and (given that) the best procedure for effecting the necessary changes.

The UBS staff received Thomson's proposal with a mixture of caution and excitement, resulting in a request for advice addressed to the UBS Board of Governors. In March 1986 the Board approved in principle "the residential-extension integration in our curriculum" and appointed a faculty Curriculum Development Committee to "monitor the restructuring of the new curriculum."[57] One of the first actions of the committee was to poll sponsors of UBS students to ascertain their reaction to the proposed changes. Responses were far from unanimous but clearly supported pursuing the project.

As a result of a prodigious amount of work by the Curriculum Development Committee, in light of a second poll of the Seminary's Board, sponsors, selected alumni, and educationists, and after lengthy discussions by the instructional staff, the original proposal was amended to retain a three-year format, incorporating a thirteen- and-a-half month internship and two half sessions at the beginning of the first and third years. In March 1987 the staff sent to the Board a recommendation that the new curriculum be approved for implementation the following June. The Board acted favorably, with a provision that the new curriculum be reviewed after three years. Incoming students were immediately informed of their need to be on the UBS campus by June 1.

Early in 1988, before the first class of students under the new curriculum was ready for internship, the Seminary added to its staff an Internship Coordinator. Through the joint efforts of the Curriculum

Development Committee and the Internship Coordinator, guidelines, job descriptions, and reporting forms were prepared. Given the originality of the program, the Seminary's initial year of internship went very well. A second class of students has recently been placed in internship locations and the original class will soon return to campus for the "Reflection Session."

Comments

Perhaps the most striking factor about UBS's implementation of its new curriculum is the fact that, by most measures, it was unnecessary. UBS presents the case of an established seminary with a recognized degree program and no shortage of students which opted for major change purely on the basis of commitment to renewal values. Theological educators who are tempted to conclude that traditional patterns preclude change in their institutions can take heart from the example of UBS. Several factors were instrumental in preparing the Seminary for the steps which were taken.

The Seminary's concern for educational outcomes must be recognized as a major source of motivation in the development of the new curriculum. The work of the Curriculum Revision Commission from 1979-1981 focused sources of dis-ease by articulating training goals in terms of qualities and competencies for ministry. The 1982 alumni study conducted by Das and the 1985 convocation of sponsors and church leaders raised additional questions which demanded response. Because the staff of the Seminary was committed to serving the church and refused to ignore evidence indicating the incumbent program was inadequately preparing students for ministry, the staff was open to change. Institutions which neglect to examine their product in terms of stated commitments cannot expect to benefit from similar motivation.

Having accepted the need for change, two values assumed major significance in shaping the direction the UBS staff looked for solutions. On the one hand, the staff candidly acknowledged that the Seminary lacked the resources needed to provide "adequate" training for ministry and sought to draw its constituent churches into partnership in the training process. This active commitment to ministry training as a shared endeavor, combining the resources of the seminary and the church, is both realistic and admirable. As the Seminary began to move toward change, the staff knew that substantive change must include significant involvement by the constituent church.

The staff was also committed to a model of ministry which combines study and service. The absence of any significant occasion to develop these disciplines in traditional seminary life was recognized to be a major deficiency. The common failure of graduates to cultivate these disciplines after leaving seminary indicates this deficiency jeopardizes the very mission of the seminary as an institution. Thus the faculty realized that significant change must present students with the opportunity and need to develop these disciplines in the course of ministry training.

Many theological educators today continue to assume that ministry preparation is the task of the seminary, and that cultivating habits necessary to sustain professional ministry is the responsibility of graduates in service. Others, concurring with the UBS staff, are prepared to share with churches the task of ministry training and to assume responsibility for guiding students into productive, life-long service. Theological faculties would do well to clarify and justify their position on these issues and to courageously implement the conclusions they reach.

Without doubt, the experience of UBS with its extension education program was also a significant precursor to change in its approach to campus training. On the one hand, the existence of materials and structures for off-campus study facilitated development of the internship program. Even more significant, however, was the staff's observation of the qualities engendered when training took place in the context of ministry. Institutions which lack experience in extension education will not share these benefits.

Finally, the presence at UBS of a catalytic personality who was willing to give expression to the issues others saw, and who was courageous enough to propose action, was certainly vital. At every point curricular development at UBS has been a team endeavor. Thompson's original proposal underwent major change in the process of dialogue within the instructional staff. One must seriously doubt, however, that any change would have been made if a call had not been sounded. Mere dissatisfaction with the status quo, and even clear identification of areas of weakness, is not enough. Those elements are present in scores of theological schools around the world. What most schools lack—and UBS enjoyed—was a person ready and willing to propose action.

It would be inappropriate to close without also noting cautions regarding the model of ministry training presented by UBS. For one thing, the Seminary has invested a vast amount of energy in development and implementation of the new curriculum. Existence of TEE texts which could serve as the basis for study in internship was a large advantage many schools lack. Even with that, the effort invested in creating this program was often matched in communicating the rationale for change to students, church leaders, and members of the Seminary Board. Seminaries which are unwilling to make a comparable investment should not enter thoughtlessly into a similar experiment.

In its first year of experience with internships UBS has also discovered that the internship experience is only as valuable as the supervisory relationship. Seminaries considering an internship requirement will do well to provide ample structure for selection, training, and support of internship supervisors.

Finally, seminaries considering internship programs should recognize that some students who otherwise qualify for admission to seminary are not ready to assume ministry responsibilities. This should not be viewed as an argument against internships, but rather as highlighting the responsibility of seminary faculty and administrators to carefully screen students admitted to theological schools.

Academic qualifications are not a reliable guide to the preparedness of students to undertake ministry training. Personal maturity, healthy interpersonal skills, spiritual vitality, servant attitudes, development of spiritual gifts, and recognition of those gifts by church leaders are factors which may correlate more directly with profitable internship experiences and effectiveness in ministry. Theological educators may need to counsel applicants lacking these qualifications to delay their entrance into seminary. There is certainly no justification for allowing immature students to experience frustration and failure in an internship placement. Besides the enormous disservice this is to the student, the church suffers as well. Adequate screening can minimize these problems, however, and enhance training effectiveness.

UBS offers a model of radical renewal of theological education. Its new curriculum, combining on-campus and off-campus study, must be considered experimental and still may be abandoned. Theological educators who are committed to the values which shaped this program, however, will be challenged by the creativity and courage of the UBS staff. Many will want to reexamine their own commitments and programs in light of this model.

Further Information

Requests for current information about UBS may be addressed to:

Dr. Brian C. Wintle, Principal
Union Biblical Seminary
Bibwewadi, Pune 411 037
Maharashtra State, India

Telephone: (91-212) 421-747

CHAPTER 11

Conservative Baptist Seminary of the East

Dresher, Pennsylvania, U.S.A.

Conservative Baptist Seminary of the East (CBSE) is a North American graduate level ministry training institution which demonstrates attentiveness to the Church, holistic curricularizing, and developmental focus. Due largely to the rigor with which these values are pursued, other renewal values are also recognizable in the program.

Description of Ministry Training at CBSE

Theological education at CBSE is conceived and undertaken as a joint venture between the seminary and local church congregations. Prior to acceptance by the seminary, the student applicant's home congregation must affirm its belief that the student is divinely called to professional Christian ministry.[58]

In the majority of cases, that congregation also serves as the principal locus of training for the seminary student.[59]

The seminary provides guidance for developing an "Internship Agreement" between the student and the "Receiving Church." The agreement includes commitment on the part of the congregation to provide two supervisors (a pastor and a lay person) to oversee the internship experience, and commitment of the student to place himself under the care and supervision of the congregation. Individual internship agreements may also include a description of specific responsibilities to be assumed by the student and provision for remuneration or scholarship assistance. The principal concern of the seminary is to assure that a meaningful internship relationship exists and to protect the interests of the student (should that become necessary).

Prior to the opening of classes each year, students and their supervisors are expected to attend an internship orientation session. Throughout the student's seminary program, the two supervisors together meet weekly with the intern to review the student's growth in character and ministry skills. To facilitate this process, the Seminary requires students to review with their supervisors a self-evaluation of their development and needs as indexed against lists of ministry skills and character traits considered desirable in a minister of the Gospel.[60]

Monthly, supervisors submit to the Seminary a log of their weekly meetings with interns which include recommendations to the student and an assessment of the level at which the student is functioning in ministry. Each student is also assigned a faculty advisor who meets weekly with his or her advisees in a group discipleship session. The student's faculty advisor is also responsible to meet with the internship supervisory team at least once each term. At the end of each term, supervisors provide written, narrative evaluation of the student's development.

In addition to monitoring and facilitating development based on the intern's involvement in congregational ministry, supervisors are requested to review with the student and to certify satisfactory completion of two learning contracts per term. The learning contracts are related to specified courses in which the student is currently enrolled and are correlated with needs identified in the self-assessment of character qualities and ministry skills.

Although the internship program is considered central to ministry training at CBSE, the Seminary is also committed to responsible academic preparation for ministry. For graduation from the three-year program,[61] students are required to satisfactorily complete sixty-six units of classroom studies, plus twenty-seven units of character and skill development covered by learning contracts. To assure academic integrity of the learning contracts, the faculty member assigned to teach the related classroom course must endorse the value of the activities included in the contract and the appropriateness of the evidences proposed. In the classroom, faculty avoid lecturing in favor of adult education methods which stress learning (vs. teaching) skills.

To preserve students' immersion in congregational ministry, classroom subjects are scheduled one day a week. Although seven or eight hours of instruction in one day admittedly is heavy, the Seminary prefers to operate on this schedule rather than diminish student involvement in the internship situation.

A traditional seminary curriculum could never be taught on one day a week, but two factors intervene in the case of CBSE.

1) Nearly 30% of credit in the curriculum (27 of 93 units) is earned through learning contracts which take advantage of a highly regarded adult education strategy but require no classroom time.
2) By running the seminary eleven months a year and offering three fifteen-week semesters annually,[62] the course load each term is reduced by a third.

Thus even full-time students are required to take only seven or eight units of classroom studies (plus three units of contracted learning) during each term. Besides preserving the congregational focus of the training program, this makes possible the one-day-per-week class schedule. It should also be noted that, due to the intensity of the program, many students choose to extend their studies over a four- or five- year period.

Students, faculty, internship (pastoral and lay) supervisors, and participating congregations are genuinely enthusiastic about this model of ministry training. Student complaints tend to focus on the intensity of the program, resulting from the comprehensive supervision of character development and ministry effectiveness in the internship setting as well as the demands of the academic schedule. Nevertheless, students attest to the value of the program in building confidence in ministry and equipping them with ministry skills.

Many of the current students are highly qualified for graduate study by any standard measure, yet have selected CBSE over traditional seminaries because of CBSE's program of church-based ministry training. It is also significant that nearly 40% of students currently enrolled at CBSE come from congregations which are not affiliated with the Conservative Baptist Association of America.[63] This is noteworthy especially since students understand that CBSE is not yet licensed to grant the Master of Divinity (M.Div.) degree.

Faculty affirm the value of CBSE's training strategy because of the opportunity provided for integration of academic studies, spiritual formation, and experience in ministry. Pastoral and lay supervisors welcome the opportunity to participate meaningfully in the preparation of pastors-in-training and report that their supervisory role has paid rich dividends in their own personal and ministry development. Some churches which have accepted interns report that the relationship has had a renewing effect on the entire congregation through the lives of the intern and the lay and pastoral supervisors.

Factors Contributing to the Development of CBSE's Approach to Ministry Training

The unique program of training for ministry at CBSE has resulted from a providential confluence of denominational loyalties, regional concern, theological conviction about the centrality of the local church, a man of high commitment and great energy, a local church which was generous in sharing their pastor, contact with and advice from a creative educator, and timely provision of prepared staff.

The dream of a Conservative Baptist seminary in the Eastern region of the United States,[64] traceable to the 1960s, provided the earliest impetus toward establishment of CBSE. Although the realization of that dream was long in coming, it was kept alive by concern over the loss of ministerial trainees from the East to the Central and Western regions. This was especially troubling in view of the immense spiritual needs of the urban, suburban, and rural areas of the Eastern Region.

An inhibiting factor was the ready availability of other denominational and interdenominational seminaries in the region. Whenever the subject of establishing a new seminary was raised, the high cost of such a project and the opportunities for traditional theological education within the region effectively argued against it.

Still, the dream would not die. Conservative Baptist pastors in the East were thankful for the training they had received at various schools, but many felt their traditional seminary experience had not prepared them well for the challenges of congregational ministry. The isolation of the academic campus from ministry involvement left them convinced that there must be a better way to prepare pastors. Their Baptist theology encouraged them to believe, furthermore, that preparation for ministry is properly a responsibility of the local church. No institution in the East provided the assistance local churches needed to undertake this task. Thus the conviction was born that a Conservative Baptist seminary could be justified if it adopted an alternative educational design.

On March 23, 1982, these conclusions were presented to messengers from forty-four Conservative Baptist churches called to receive the report of a Seminary Feasibility Committee formed three years before. At that meeting the messengers voted to constitute a provisional Board of Trustees to implement the proposal presented by the committee.

It is significant that the chairman of the Feasibility Committee was Rev. Glenn Blossom, pastor of Chelten Baptist Church, in the Philadelphia suburb of Dresher, Pennsylvania. In October 1983, Rev. Blossom was named the first president of the new seminary. Prior to his own theological studies, Blossom had served on the staff of South Baptist Church, Lansing, Michigan, with university professor Ted Ward.

In the course of the Feasibility Committee's deliberations, and more intensively after Blossom's appointment as president, Ward and his associates were involved as consultants to the new seminary. As the Board worked out the educational philosophy and policies of the seminary, Blossom's energetic commitment to the concept of CBSE stirred the vision in others and generated critical funding for the project. The willingness of Chelten Baptist Church to allow Pastor Blossom to promote CBSE and serve as the Seminary's first president at that time must be viewed as an important factor in the development of the seminary.

In February 1985, Drs. James Mignard (Dean) and F. David Spruance (Associate Dean) took their places as the first full-time faculty of the Seminary. Mignard, who holds a Ph.D. in New Testament and has done extensive post-graduate studies in adult education, came from an active career as a consultant to medical educators. Spruance had served for thirty-one years in Argentina as evangelist, theological educator, and director of Conservative Baptist mission work in that nation. Together they tackled the task of translating dreams, philosophy, and policies into a program of training.

Mignard's background in adult education was formative. Spruance, who was assigned responsibility to develop the internship program, was deeply influenced by Professor Doran McCarty of Golden Gate Theological Seminary. McCarty's book, *The Supervision of Ministry Students*,[65] attendance at a timely seminar offered by McCarty in San Francisco, and personal contacts with McCarty during and after the seminar provided the initial framework of the CBSE internship program. To provide guidance for the developing seminary, the faculty consulted with Conservative Baptist pastors and laymen in the region. In two meetings with church leaders, lists of ministerial skills and character traits desirable in a pastor were compiled for use by the faculty.

When the first classes were held, in September 1985, the essential form of the new seminary was already established. Subsequent faculty and other individuals have certainly made significant contributions, but the basic approach to ministry training, and the principles which shape training at CBSE, have not been altered.

Those most closely related to the Seminary are satisfied that four years' experience has proven the wisdom of commitments made before the school was born. Indeed, faculty and students, internship supervisors and participating congregations all seem to agree that the CBSE formula for pastoral preparation represents an effective approach to training for ministry. It will be interesting to observe CBSE over the next couple of decades to see what adaptations are made and how graduates and their churches evaluate their preparation for ministry.

Observations

A critical factor in the apparent success of CBSE, not previously mentioned, is the fact that the model of training described was adopted from the beginning of the Seminary. This provided the opportunity to do something new without consideration of tenured faculty with specific professional expectations or of real and tangible properties entailing overhead and maintenance. This is to say that the CBSE model of training for ministry is probably unsuitable for adoption by an established Bible school or seminary.

There are several elements of the CBSE experiment, nonetheless, which may be transferable in some form. Other institutions can adopt adult learning methods in preference to nearly exclusive use of lecture instruction.[66] Specifically, other institutions may want to experiment with use of learning contracts (with academic credit) for development of ministry skills and Christian character.

Much of the internship structure, with its involvement of pastoral and lay supervisors, could be incorporated into other ministry training programs, even though those programs retain a traditional campus-oriented structure. Institutions considering such a commitment should be very realistic, however, concerning the personnel resources required to launch and sustain such a program.

Note that each student must have an internship church, and each church must agree to provide two supervisors—one a member of the pastoral staff of the congregation, and one an active lay person. These supervisors, furthermore, must commit themselves to meaningful involvement and investment in the life of the intern. (Weekly supervisory meetings under CBSE's internship program are scheduled for one hour, but often run longer. Meeting preparation, logs, narrative reports, and informal involvement with the intern, of course, is in addition to time allocated for weekly meetings.)

To guide and equip supervisors in this strategic ministry, the seminary must provide regular (perhaps monthly) meaningful opportunities for training, questions, and interaction. Furthermore, a member of the seminary's faculty must assume responsibility for each student, meeting weekly with advisees in the Discipleship session, and at least once each term with each intern's supervisory team. This procedure is extremely labor intensive. It is the close cooperation between the seminary and the internship congregation, however, which has proven especially developmental for CBSE students. Attempts to implement a modified internship program which demands more limited investment by the seminary and the internship congregation cannot be expected to produce the same results.

Those familiar with traditional seminary education may observe that CBSE lacks the academic rigor usually associated with pastoral training. This reflects a deliberate choice on the part of the faculty to reallocate the sources of (orchestrated) stress in the life of the student. The faculty recognizes that elevated stress can facilitate learning and development, but excessive stress results in frustration, despair, and burnout. Because CBSE is committed to substantial development of the student's character and ministry skills, as well as theological understanding, the Seminary has chosen to place major emphasis on the internship program. The student's close supervision in the internship program produces immense stress (often leaving him no place to hide) but has also proven to be very developmental. To avoid student burnout, however, it has been necessary to reduce stresses generated in classroom instruction.

Two factors protect the integrity of academic instruction at CBSE:

1) Traditional theological disciplines

These disciplines—including Biblical, historical, theological, pastoral, and mission studies—are included in the seminary curriculum. The Seminary's faculty members are well qualified and take seriously their responsibility for the theological formation of students.

2) Adoption of adult education strategies

Such strategies allow CBSE to realize maximum learning outcomes for faculty and student time invested. The students' intensive involvement in ministry during studies is fully exploited through reflective interaction on classroom and internship experiences. By assigning students a significant role in the teaching-learning process, furthermore, learning becomes more meaningful and patterns are established which can guide continued study and development.

CBSE's decision to reapportion priorities in ministry training must be viewed in terms of the Seminary's conviction that substantially greater attention must be given to the spiritual and ministry formation of seminarians. Others may not share this conviction. On the other hand, if other faculties are persuaded that Biblical and theological qualifications for pastoral ministry go beyond the knowledge and skills acquired through academic requirements, they may want to review their own training goals and strategies. When a faculty has come to grips with the limits of developmental stress and the consequent need to attenuate rigor in one dimension of training in order to increase focus on another, the stage will be set for significant dialogue.

Finally, other seminaries could adopt an eleven-month academic calendar and schedule classes on only one day per week. These innovations will only be attractive, however, to institutions which share CBSE's profound commitment to returning the focus of ministry training to the local church. Some may feel that preparation for ministry is best undertaken by a professional faculty in an academic community. If others conclude on theological grounds that ministry preparation properly belongs in the local congregation, they clearly must explore the implications of that conviction for theological education structures and strategies.

Further Information

Requests for current information about CBSE may be addressed to:

Dr. John F. Robinson, President
Conservative Baptist Seminary of the East
Post Office Box 611
Dresher, PA 19025

Telephone: (215) 646-3322

CHAPTER 12

Looking Back And Looking Ahead

As the preceding chapters document, new models of ministry training are emerging in many parts of the world. Renewal of theological education is occurring. Yet the cases reported have all developed in isolation, each the result of one institution's—sometimes one individual's—commitment to respond more Biblically and more creatively to the challenge of training men and women for ministry. Other cases could be added to this collection, and in that we take heart. In no case has renewal touched every aspect of a training institution, however, nor has it occurred uniformly. Realism reminds us that in most evangelical theological schools around the world, renewal is only a dream, a thirst (often ill-defined) as yet unsatisfied.

Factors Common to Selected Schools

As I traveled around the world to visit the schools described above, I watched for constants—factors which occurred in several (if not all) of the institutions I visited. I recognize that educational models developed in Philadelphia or Jos or Pune or Adelaide may not transfer well to another situation, but perhaps factors exist which characterize institutions committed to renewal of theological education. If so, then these may provide insight for administrators who desire to see renewal of ministry training in their own institutions.

I have identified seven factors which consistently reappear across the institutions I visited. As this research is extended to other schools, the following list may be expanded or narrowed. I offer these observations, however, for reflection and discussion.

All selected schools have a strong missions emphasis
This observation surprised me, since missiological orientation was not a factor in institutional selection. Perhaps I would have been less surprised had I remembered that the initiatives that gave rise to the Theological Education Fund and Theological Education by Extension originated in missions contexts. Nevertheless, ten out of ten schools I visited incorporate a strong emphasis on equipping students for missionary outreach.

Other schools evidence missionary commitment similar to those included in this study, yet renewal is not evident on their campuses. Emphasis on missions apparently is not an adequate cause of renewal in theological education.

There are factors in missionary orientation and experience, however, which are favorable to renewal. Effective cross-cultural ministers are highly goal oriented, are sensitive to the feedback systems of their context, and are able to adopt unfamiliar means to obtain mission goals. Perhaps it is not coincidental that some of the most creative innovations in ministry training have been pioneered by missionary educators.

Renewal of ministry training is embraced and promoted by the chief executive officer (principal, president, or dean)
I did not observe any exception to this rule. Revolution may originate from below, but renewal seems to prosper only when it is endorsed and promoted from the top.

The central role of leadership in renewal may arise from the level of corporate commitment required to achieve renewal, it may reflect the CEO's capacity to establish a climate favorable (or hostile) to creativity and change, or it may be necessary for meaningful assessment of institutional achievement and objectives. Whatever the mechanisms, any institution is fortunate to have leadership committed to appropriate and effective training for ministry.

Principals and deans who desire renewal in their institutions will find specific suggestions below. Many schools, however, lack that kind of leadership. Faculty and board members of those schools will be wise to win institutional leaders to the cause of renewal. Every effort should be taken to avoid bypassing or undercutting the leadership structure of the institution. Prayerful proposal or implementation of strategies suggested below may be used by God to arouse Biblical concern for ministry training.

Careful attention is given to the school's constituent church and its training needs

This quality was more uneven, but most clearly manifest at Canadian Theological Seminary, Conservative Baptist Seminary of the East, and the African and Asian schools. In Western interdenominational institutions, such as Columbia Bible College and Seminary and Bibelschule Brake, constituent sensitivity assumes a non-ecclesiastical expression.

It should not amaze us that renewal of theological education correlates with orientation to the training needs of a constituent church. Every institution assumes a fundamental orientation, and "service of the church" has long been the professed purpose of theological schools. Any willingness to allow that purpose to shape the design of training programs affords an encouraging— and soul searching—alternative to the more common orientation to academia.

Focus is placed on training outcomes (i.e., the effectiveness of graduates in ministry) with freedom to adapt programs and processes to improve graduate effectiveness

Canadian Theological Seminary provides a model for outcomes assessment, but a willingness to look at the effectiveness of graduates in ministry is characteristic of all institutions included in the study. Dissatisfaction with the school's product was a principal stimulus toward change at All Nations Christian College and Union Biblical Seminary. Conservative Baptist Seminary of the East, Jos ECWA Theological Seminary, and China Graduate School of Theology reviewed the product of traditional seminaries and determined they wanted to do better.

A well-designed and objectively executed outcomes assessment is an effective antidote to naive assumptions about a school's product. Realism about the strengths and weaknesses of a school's alumni can provide strong motivation toward more effective and appropriate training. When this drive was empowered by freedom to innovate, the schools in this study experienced renewal.

Conscious effort is directed toward spiritual formation and ministry skills development, sometimes with deliberate attenuation of academic stress

All of the schools included in the study evidenced this quality, although none more dramatically than Union Biblical Seminary and Conservative Baptist Seminary of the East.

Since spiritual formation and ministry skills development are both renewal values, this pattern should have been expected. I was not prepared to find this focus in all schools, however, nor had I anticipated the rigor with which it is pursued.

Although none of the schools in this study has discounted the need for sound academic training, the relative emphasis on spiritual and ministerial skills development in some cases gives that impression. This stems from realistic recognition of the limits of developmental stress. The principal source of stress in traditional theological education is academic. When spiritual and ministry skills development are accorded higher priority, new sources of stress are introduced. To avoid student overload and burnout, some schools have taken the bold (but reasonable) step of deliberately reapportioning stress. My amazement, I concluded, reflects failure to anticipate the programmatic implications of refocusing spiritual and ministry development.

Faculty make themselves vulnerable to students through individual and small group mentoring and through involvement with students in ministry

This factor also was unevenly evidenced. Intense mentoring is a central aspect of training at Conservative Baptist Seminary of the East and All Nations Christian College. At Bibelschule Brake and Bible College of South Australia faculty regularly lead student teams in evangelistic outreach.

This factor also surprised me, although it should not have. On the one hand, it is a reasonable extension of a Biblical emphasis on the teacher as model. On the other hand, it reverses a well-established but counterproductive pattern of distancing between faculty and students. It also affords the only truly persuasive denial of an unbiblical separation of knowing and doing, understanding and obedience.

Administrators and faculty are aware of adult education principles and design instruction for adult learners

Adult educators played major roles in shaping training at Jos ECWA Theological Seminary, Bible College of South Australia, Union Biblical Seminary, Conservative Baptist Seminary of the East, and Canadian Theological Seminary.

It is encouraging to observe the impact of adult education principles on ministry training. Some institutions turned to educational consultants in their search for more effective training, while educators within other institutions were catalysts of renewal. Failure to consider contact with adult education theory in selection of institutional case studies makes its commonness even more impressive.

Some of these "constants" reflect implementation of renewal values, while others suggest fundamental changes in the way we go about training for ministry. Most of those changes are threatening and involve risk. Nevertheless, I am optimistic. We have seen that theological educators desire renewal; they recognize that renewal values are appropriate and Biblical. We now have evidence that change is possible, that others are experiencing the renewal many desire. Renewal of theological education, personally and institutionally, deserves the support of every theological educator. With the data in hand, every reason exists to expect renewal to flourish.

Suggestions for Promoting Institutional Renewal

Renewal is not flourishing in most evangelical schools, however. Most ministry training institutions are locked into traditional patterns which belie our hopes for something better. I invite administrators, faculty, and board members of those institutions to appoint themselves agents of renewal in their setting. The following comments are addressed to those who accept this invitation.

My basic proposal is this: Renewal must be viewed as an ongoing quest to make ministry training more Biblical, not as a fad or a "technique" for solving urgent problems. This quest, furthermore, requires the participation and support of every member of the training community. For that reason those who seek renewal cannot afford to alienate or ignore any member of the theological school's faculty or board; each one must be courted prayerfully and won. "Renewal" which is imposed by fiat, furthermore, denies the values it seeks to promote. A more effective approach is to demonstrate that renewal values are Biblically valid and educationally sound.

To this end, I offer ten specific suggestions. These do not constitute a formula for renewal of theological education (since every institution is unique and renewal cannot be programmed). It is, rather, a list of factors which have contributed to renewal in other contexts. Where they are not immediately applicable, I trust they will prove suggestive.

Promote open communication linkages with the constituent church

If the purpose of the theological school is to serve the church, then open channels of communication between church and school are imperative. This may take an inauspicious form, such as inviting local clergymen and elders to participate in (critique?) an individual class. Or it may assume a formal structure, such as appointing a "pastors' advisory committee to the principal (or dean)." Dialogues between faculty and churchmen may be scheduled, sometimes with preset topics and at others with the agenda open. Pastors and leading lay persons may be invited to participate in faculty meetings and sit on faculty committees (perhaps initially as guests or observers, but soon as full participants and peers).

For some institutions, the first challenge will be to identify in specific and realistic terms the church constituency they seek to serve. Even if the school serves a broad constituency, there is merit in identifying a "central core" to which the administration and faculty can relate.

Because theological educators are not accustomed to sharing control of training institutions, resistance to these suggestions may be anticipated. If resisted, the issue should not be forced. Instead, administrators and faculty may be encouraged to collectively reflect on the Biblical meaning of servanthood as preparation for establishing communication linkages with the church at a later date.

Undertake an outcomes study

Many ministry training institutions poll graduates regarding their experience on campus. Polls directed only to current students and recent graduates, however, have limited value for curriculum development. Unless polling instruments are well designed and data appropriately analyzed, furthermore, findings may be meaningless or misleading.

A carefully developed outcomes study, on the other hand, can provide a stimulating beginning point for faculty, board, and constituent church reflection on institutional purposes and programs. To be used this way, however, the participant bodies should be involved in the design and interpretation of the study, not only in discussing its implications.[67]

Circulate literature on renewal to members of the faculty and board

The ICAA "Manifesto on Renewal of Evangelical Theological Education" provides the basis for many substantive discussions, although it may not be the best place to begin. Several of the articles cited in Chapter One may be more useful for introducing the challenge of renewal, especially if educators are not dissatisfied with traditional training patterns. For many institutions, Farley's *Theologia* can focus discussion at an intermediate level.

Since the school's board of control can effectively support or thwart movement toward renewal, it is important to include board members at each stage of sensitization and dialogue. Although this may protract the renewal process, administrators and faculty cannot afford to move far ahead of board members and the constituent church. Those who do, belie their commitment to leadership as servanthood and risk rejection of renewal proposals by board and church leaders.

Provide training in adult education theory and methods for members of the faculty and board

A series of one-day faculty retreats could be invaluable in orienting instructors to adult education theory and in facilitating modification of syllabi and class plans. If no one at the school has the required expertise, it may be worth obtaining the services of an adult educator.

An even more basic need, however, is to develop literacy in adult education among members of the faculty and board. The reading lists included in Chapter Ten may prove helpful to this end. Knowles' Modern Practice of Adult Education launched a new era in adult education, but works by Brookfield, Daloz, and Knox reflect more recent developments in the field. New release lists from Jossey-Bass Publishers can be useful in identifying current theory and practice.

Focus the role of faculty as models

One of the most sobering moments in the life of an instructor comes when we recognize that we reproduce ourselves in our students. Jesus stated the issue baldly in Luke 6:40.

Our Lord's most pointed instruction on the qualifications of teachers, however, is found in Matthew 23:1-12. Lack of consistency in doctrine and life (v. 3), lack of compassion (v. 4), and lack of humility (vv. 5-7) disqualify one to serve as a teacher in Christ's Church. Indeed, those qualified to teach do not set themselves above their students (v. 8), they do not ascribe allegiance to human teachers—contemporary or historic (v. 9), and they do not gather disciples to themselves (v. 10). The passage concludes with a warning against elitism and a call to humility (vv. 11-12). These principles are important because they reflect the way Christ teaches us; they are also important because we imprint our attitudes, values, and relationships on our students.

Assure the commitment and support of the chief executive officer

As noted above, leadership of the principal or dean appears crucial to achieving renewal of theological education in any institution. If the chief executive officer is not open to pursuit of renewal despite responsible efforts to raise renewal concerns, institutional progress toward renewal should be deferred. Those who seek renewal may still pursue renewal values and strategies in their own instructional roles and relationships. They can also intercede regularly and urgently for God's renewing grace in their institution and its leadership.

Cultivate an atmosphere of experimentation

Improvement necessarily involves change, change comes only through experimentation, and experimentation entails risk. Risk taking commonly occurs, however, only in contexts of desperation or security. Few theological educators—administrators and instructors—so keenly feel the need for renewal of ministry training as to be pushed to experiment with new strategies for developing church leaders. Traditional patterns are established, accepted, and safe.

If we are to achieve any major improvement in ministry training effectiveness, therefore, boards, administrators, and faculties must provide the security and encouragement needed to support experimentation. Even small experiments (e.g., employing adult education strategies in a single class) should be publicized and promoted. Experiments will not always have happy endings. When experimentation is informed by sound doctrine and responsible educational principles, however, negative experiences will never be disastrous. It is this confidence that frees administrators and faculty colleagues to encourage experiments toward renewal of ministry training.

Circulate case studies on renewal

The global survey of theological educators reported in Chapter Three showed that many affirm renewal values and desire renewal in their institutions but are unaware of others who have achieved major strides toward renewal. Chapters Four through Eleven of this booklet seek to remedy that lack. I trust this will spur an avalanche of articles reporting experiments at other institutions seeking to implement renewal values in a variety of contexts. Until more articles appear, the previous chapters may serve to apprise educators of proven alternative strategies and to expand the range of experimentation.

One caution: Because each institution is unique, innovations introduced in one context can rarely be replicated successfully in another. The challenge is not to adopt a model developed in another school. Each faculty, rather, should explore implications for their own institution of insights and principles embodied in the models reported.

Clarify training goals

Most theological schools have goal statements of some kind. Although these statements vary greatly in form and content, they fall naturally into two classes—those written by an individual or adopted from another source, and those developed corporately by the school's administrators, faculty, and constituent church. In both cases, the goal statement is worth less than the process by which it was produced. Corporate development (or review and revision) of an institutional goals statement can provide an ideal context for exploring shared values and reassessing commitments.

I believe any attempt to think strategically about ministry training should begin with a careful review of the nature of the church. As I understand the Scriptures, God intends the church to be a worshiping, nurturing, redemptive, and witnessing community. A biblical ecclesiology provides the necessary context for understanding the nature of leadership in the church. A biblical theology of church leadership, in turn, is prerequisite to meaningful discussion of the role of the theological school and the goals of theological education. Failure to pursue this approach easily leads to divergent conclusions by churchmen and scholars, and polarization of the faculty along professional disciplines.

If our institutions equip leaders who, in turn, equip the saints for ministry (cf. Eph 4:12), who are agents of Christ's kingdom in their communities (cf. 2 Tim 4:1-2), and who share God's sacrificial love for a lost world (cf. Jn 3;16), we can be sure we have not missed the mark by far.

Corporately reexamine structural and curricular commitments

Reflection on renewal values and institutional goals will have little use unless we confront the implications for ministry training at our own schools. Some faculties will be able only to consider incremental change. Other faculties, dissatisfied with the limitations of traditional models and attracted by reports of creative change at other schools, will be open to more fundamental adjustments. Not only instructional methods and curricular design will be reexamined, but also training structures, including the roles and relationships of church and school, or teachers and students.

A final caution is in order. Change for the sake of change is rarely constructive. Renewal is guided by biblical values and sound educational principles. Nevertheless, when prayerful reexamination of commitments indicates change is in order, faith will not hold back. By God's grace and guidance theological education can be renewed. Ministry training institutions can serve the Church more adequately. May God grant wisdom to all who seek to be faithful to this calling, for the sake of Christ and his Church.

Appendices

ICAA Manifesto on the Renewal of Evangelical Theological Education
June 1983

The fundamental presupposition of the "Manifesto" is the perception that today there is a wide agreement among evangelical theological educators on the need for renewal in theological education and on an agenda for such renewal. The strategic purpose of the "Manifesto" itself is to reinforce this agreement and give it a cutting edge by a vivid and forceful assertion of its essential points. For just this reason the "Manifesto" is not meant to express everything that might need changing, but only those leading points on which there appears to be wide consent. Through the "Manifesto" ICAA seeks to declare publicly its commitment to renewal and gain for itself and others a visible sense of direction in pursuing such renewal.

Introduction

We who serve within evangelical theological education throughout the world today, and who find ourselves now linked together in growing international cooperation, wish to give united voice to our longing and prayer for the renewal of evangelical theological education today—for a renewal in form and in substance, a renewal in vision and power, a renewal in commitment and direction.

We rightly seek such renewal in light of the pivotal significance of theological education in biblical perspective. Insofar as theological education concerns the formation of leadership for the church of Christ in its mission, to that extent theological education assumes a critically strategic biblical importance. Scripture mandates the church, it mandates leadership service within that church, and it thereby as well mandates a vital concern with the formation of such leadership. For this reason the quest for effective renewal in evangelical theological education in our day is a biblically generated quest.

We rightly seek such renewal in light also of the crisis of leadership upon the church of Christ around the world. The times are weighted with unusual challenge and unusual opportunity, demanding of the Church exceptional preparation of its leadership. In many areas the church is faced with surging growth of such proportions that it cannot always cope. In many areas the church is also faced with open hostility without and hidden subversion within, distracting and diverting it from its calling. Everywhere the opportunities and challenges take on new and confusing forms. The times demand an urgent quest for the renewal of theological education patterns, that the church in its leadership may be equipped to fulfill its high calling under God.

We rightly seek such renewal also in light of the condition of evangelical theological education in our day. We recognize among ourselves exciting examples of that renewed vitality in theological education which we desire to see everywhere put to the service of our Lord. Things are being done right, within traditional patterns and within nontraditional patterns, which need attention, encouragement and emulation. We also recognize that there are examples in our midst, usually all too close at hand, where things are not being done right. We confess this with shame. Traditional forms are being maintained only because they are traditional, and radical forms pursued only because they are radical—and the formation of effective leadership for the church of Christ is deeply hindered. We heartily welcome the wise critiques of evangelical theological education which have arisen in recent times, which have forced us to think much more carefully both about our purposes in theological education and about the best means for achieving those purposes. We believe that there is now emerging around the world a wide consensus among evangelical theological educators that a challenge to renewal is upon us, and upon us from our Lord. We believe that there is also emerging a broad agreement on the central patterns that such a renewal should take. New times are upon us, and new opportunities. We wish to pursue these opportunities, and seize them, in obedience to the Lord.

Therefore, in order to provide encouragement, guidance, and critical challenge to ourselves and to all others who may look to us for direction, we wish to assert and endorse the following agenda for the renewal of evangelical theological education worldwide today, and to pledge ourselves to its practical energetic implementation. We do not pretend to ourselves that we are here setting forth either a full or a final word on these matters. But we do make this expression after extended prayerful reflection, and we wish to offer the hand of warm friendship to all those who may likewise feel led to endorse these proposals, and express to them an invitation to practical collaboration in this quest, for the sake of Jesus Christ our Lord, the evangelization of the world, and the establishment and edification of the church.

Therefore, we now unitedly affirm that, to fulfill its God-given mandate, evangelical theological education today worldwide must vigorously seek to introduce and reinforce—

Contextualization

Our programs of theological education must be designed with deliberate reference to the contexts in which they serve. We are at fault that our curricula so often appear either to have been imported whole from abroad, or to have been handed down unaltered from the past. The selection of courses for the curriculum, and the content of every course in the curriculum, must be specifically suited to the context of service. To become familiar with the context in which the biblical message is to be lived and preached is no less vital to a well-rounded program than to become familiar with the content of that biblical message. Indeed, not only in what is taught, but also in structure and operation our theological programs must demonstrate that they exist in and for their own specific context, in governance and administration, in staffing and finance, in teaching styles and class assignments, in library resources and student services. This we must accomplish, by God's grace.

Churchward orientation

Our programs of theological education must orient themselves pervasively in terms of the Christian community being served. We are at fault when our programs operate merely in terms of some traditional or personal notion of theological education. At every level of design and operation our programs must be visibly determined by a close attentiveness to the needs and expectations of the Christian community we serve. To this end we must establish multiple modes of ongoing contact and interaction between program and church, both at official and at grassroots levels, and regularly adjust and develop the program in light of these contacts. Our theological programs must become manifestly of the church, through the church, and for the church. This we must accomplish, by God's grace.

Strategic flexibility

Our programs of theological education must nurture a much greater strategic flexibility in carrying out their task. Too long we have been content to serve the formation of only one type of leader for the church, at only one level of need, by only one educational approach. If we are to serve fully the leadership needs of the body of Christ, then our programs, singly and in combination, must begin to demonstrate much greater flexibility in at least three respects.

Firstly, we must attune ourselves to the full range of leadership roles required, and not attend only to the most familiar or most basic. To provide for pastoral formation, for example, is not enough. We must respond creatively, in cooperation with other programs, to the church's leadership needs also in areas such as Christian education, youth work, evangelism, journalism and communications, TEE, counseling, denominational and parachurch administration, seminary and Bible school staffing, community development, and social outreach.

Secondly, our programs must learn to take account of all academic levels of need, and not become frozen in serving only one level. We must not presume that the highest level of training is the only strategic need, nor conversely that the lowest level is the only strategic need. We must deliberately participate in multilevel approaches to leadership training, worked out on the basis of an assessment of the church's leadership needs as a whole at all levels.

Thirdly, we must embrace a greater flexibility in the educational modes by which we touch the various levels of leadership need, and not limit our approach to a single traditional or radical pattern. We must learn to employ, in practical combination with others, both residential and extension systems, both formal and nonformal styles, as well, for example, as short-term courses, workshops, night school programs, vacation institutes, in-service training, traveling seminars, refresher courses and continuing education programs. Only by such flexibility in our programs can the church's full spectrum of leadership needs begin to be met and we ourselves become true to our full mandate. This we must accomplish, by God's grace.

Theological grounding

Evangelical theological education as a whole today needs earnestly to pursue and recover a thorough-going theology of theological education. We are at fault that we so readily allow our bearings to be set for us by the latest enthusiasms, or by secular rationales, or by sterile traditions. It is not sufficient that we attend to the context of our service and to the Christian community being served. We must come to perceive our task, and even these basic points of reference, within the larger setting of God's total truth and God's total plan. Such a shared theological perception of our calling is largely absent from our midst. We must together take immediate and urgent steps to seek, elaborate, and possess a biblically informed theological basis for our calling in theological education and allow every aspect of our service to become rooted and nurtured in this soil. This we must accomplish, by God's grace.

Continuous assessment

Our programs of theological education must be dominated by a rigorous practice of identifying objectives, assessing outcomes, and adjusting programs accordingly. We have been too easily satisfied with educational intentions that are unexpressed, or only superficially examined, or too general to be of directional use. We have been too ready to assume our achievements on the basis of vague impressions, chance reports, or crisis-generated inquiries. We have been culpably content with evaluating our programs only irregularly, or haphazardly, or under stress. We hear our Lord's stern word of the faithful stewardship he requires in his servants, but we have largely failed to apply this to the way we conduct our programs of theological education.

Firstly, we must let our programs become governed by objectives carefully chosen, clearly defined, and continuously reviewed. Secondly, we must accept it as a duty, and not merely as beneficial, to discern and evaluate the results of our programs, so that there may be a valid basis for judging the degree to which intentions are being achieved. This requires that we institute means for reviewing the actual performance of our graduates in relation to our stated objectives. Thirdly, we must build into the normal operational patterns of our programs a regular review and continual modification and adjustment of all aspects of governance, staffing, educational program, facilities, and student service, so that actual achievements might be brought to approximate more and more closely our stated objectives. Only by such provisions for continuous assessment can we be true to the rigorous demands of biblical stewardship. This we must accomplish, by God's grace.

Community life

Our programs of theological education must demonstrate the Christian pattern of community. We are at fault that our programs so often seem little more than Christian academic factories, efficiently producing graduates. It is biblically incumbent on us that our programs function as deliberately nurtured Christian educational communities, sustained by those modes of community that are biblically commended and culturally appropriate. To this end it is not merely decorative but biblically essential that the whole educational body—staff and students— not only learn together, but play and eat and care and worship and work together. This we must accomplish, by God's grace.

Integrated program

Our programs of theological education must combine spiritual and practical with academic objectives in one holistic integrated educational approach. We are at fault that we so often focus educational requirements narrowly on cognitive attainments, while we hope for student growth in other dimensions but leave it largely to chance. Our programs must be designed to attend to the growth and equipping of the whole man of God.

This means, firstly, that our educational programs must deliberately seek and expect the spiritual formation of the student. We must look for a spiritual development centered in total commitment to the lordship of Christ, progressively worked outward by the power of the Spirit into every department of life. We must devote as much time and care and structural designing to facilitate this type of growth as we readily and rightly provide for cognitive growth.

This also means, secondly, that our programs must seek and expect achievement in the practical skills of Christian leadership. We must not any longer only introduce these skills within a classroom setting. We must incorporate into our educational arrangements and requirements a guided practical field experience in precisely those skills which the student will need to employ in service after completion of the program. We must provide adequately supervised and monitored opportunities for practical vocational field experiences. We must blend practical and spiritual with academic in our educational programs, and thus equip the whole man of God for service. This we must accomplish, by God's grace.

Servant molding

Through our programs of theological education students must be molded to styles of leadership appropriate to their intended biblical role within the body of Christ. We are to be blamed that our programs so readily produce the characteristics of elitism and so rarely produce the characteristics of servanthood. We must not merely hope that the true marks of Christian servanthood will appear. We must actively promote biblically approved styles of leadership through modeling by the staff and through active encouragement, practical exposition, and deliberate reinforcement. This we must accomplish, by God's grace.

Instructional variety

Our programs of theological education must vigorously pursue the use of a variety of educational teaching methodologies, evaluated and promoted in terms of their demonstrated effectiveness, especially with respect to the particular cultural context. It is not right to become fixed in one method merely because it is traditional, or familiar, or even avant-garde. Lecturing is by no means the only appropriate teaching method, and frequently by no means the best. Presumably neither is programmed instruction. Our programs need to take practical steps to introduce and train their staff in new methods of instruction, in a spirit of innovative flexibility and experimentation, always governed by the standard of effectiveness.

A Christian mind

Our programs of theological education need much more effectively to model and inculcate a pattern of holistic thought that is openly and wholesomely centered around biblical truth as the integrating core of reality. It is not enough merely to teach an accumulation of theological truths. Insofar as every human culture is governed at its core by an integrating world view, our programs must see that the rule of our Lord is planted effectively at that point in the life of the student. This vision of the theologically integrated life needs to be so lived and taught in our programs that we may say and show in a winsomely biblical manner that theology does indeed matter, and students may go forth experiencing this centering focus in all its biblical richness and depth. This we must accomplish, by God's grace.

Equipping for growth

Our programs of theological education need urgently to refocus their patterns of training toward encouraging and facilitating self-directed learning. It is not enough that through our programs we bring a student to a state of preparedness for ministry. We need to design academic requirements so that we are equipping the student not only to complete the course but also for a lifetime of ongoing learning and development and growth. To this end we must also assume a much greater role in the placement of our students, as part of our proper duty, and experiment in ways of maintaining ongoing supportive links and services with the student after graduation, especially in the early years of ministry. By these means each student should come to experience through the program not the completion of a development but the launching of an ongoing development. This we must accomplish, by God's grace.

Cooperation

Our programs of theological education must pursue contact and collaboration among themselves for mutual support, encouragement, edification, and cross-fertilization. We are at fault that so often in evangelical theological education we attend merely to our own assignments under God. Others in the same calling need us, and we need them. The biblical notion of mutuality needs to be much more visibly expressed and pragmatically pursued among our theological programs. Too long we have acquiesced in an isolation of effort that denies the larger body of Christ, thus failing both ourselves and Christ's body. The times in which we serve, no less than biblical expectations, demand of each of us active ongoing initiatives in cooperation. This we must accomplish, by God's grace.

MAY GOD HELP US TO BE FAITHFUL TO THESE AFFIRMA-TIONS AND COMMITMENTS, TO THE GLORY OF GOD AND FOR THE FULFILLMENT OF HIS PURPOSE.

Questionnaire for ICAA Member Agencies

Instructions: Your prompt response to this questionnaire will be much appreciated. When alternative responses are offered, circle the letter closest to your opinion. Please reflect your own experience or opinion in responding to the following questions.

1. Would you say you are familiar with the ICAA "Manifesto on the Renewal of Evangelical Theological Education"?

    A. Very Familiar   C. Slightly Familiar

    B. Somewhat Familiar   D. Unfamiliar

2. What do you perceive to be the purpose of the "Manifesto"? What ends does it seek to promote?

    _____

    _____

    _____

    _____

3.   Please list the most important points from the "Manifesto," as you
      recall them.

_____   _____

_____   _____

_____   _____

_____   _____

*The "Manifesto" is based on the perception that today there is a wide agreement
among evangelical theological educators on the need for renewal in theological
education.*

4.   Do you agree that there is need for renewal in evangelical theologi-
      cal education?

             A. Strongly Agree   C. Doubtful

             B. Somewhat Agree   D. Strongly Disagree

5.   If you affirm a need for renewal in theological education, what
      specifically do you intend to affirm? What changes do you feel are
      needed to renew theological education?

_____

_____

_____

_____

_____

The ICAA "Manifesto" presents an agenda for the renewal of theological education consisting of twelve points. In the following section, those points are presented with questions about your observations and opinions. On each scale, circle the number which best reflects your view.

6.   **Contextualization**—*Our programs of theological education must be designed with deliberate reference to the contexts in which they serve.*

Do theological schools in your region already demonstrate this quality to a high degree?

        None do   All do

              1   2   3   4   5   6   7

What priority would you assign to efforts to change this aspect of theological education within your region?

        Unimportant   Highest Priority

              1   2   3   4   5   6   7

7.   **Churchward orientation**—*Our programs of theological education must orient themselves pervasively in terms of the Christian community being served.*

Do theological schools in your region already demonstrate this quality to a high degree?

        None do   All do

              1   2   3   4   5   6   7

What priority would you assign to efforts to change this aspect of theological education within your region?

        No Priority   Highest Priority

              1   2   3   4   5   6   7

8.   **Strategic flexibility**—*Our programs of theological education must be prepared to nurture church leaders for various roles, at various levels, and through various modes of training.*

Do theological schools in your region already demonstrate this quality to a high degree?

None do   All do

1   2   3   4   5   6   7

What priority would you assign to efforts to change this aspect of theological education within your region?

No Priority   Highest Priority

1   2   3   4   5   6   7

9.   **Theological grounding**—*Evangelical theological education needs earnestly to recover a thorough-going theology of theological education.*

Do theological schools in your region already demonstrate this quality to a high degree?

None do   All do

1   2   3   4   5   6   7

What priority would you assign to efforts to change this aspect of theological education within your region?

No Priority   Highest Priority

1   2   3   4   5   6   7

10. **Continuous assessment**—*Our programs of theological education must be dominated by a rigorous practice of identifying objectives, assessing outcomes, and adjusting programs accordingly.*

Do theological schools in your region already demonstrate this quality to a high degree?

None do   All do

       1   2   3   4   5   6   7

What priority would you assign to efforts to change this aspect of theological education within your region?

No Priority   Highest Priority

       1   2   3   4   5   6   7

11. **Community life**—*Our programs of theological education must demonstrate the Christian pattern of community.*

Do theological schools in your region already demonstrate this quality to a high degree?

None do   All do

       1   2   3   4   5   6   7

What priority would you assign to efforts to change this aspect of theological education within your region?

No Priority   Highest Priority

       1   2   3   4   5   6   7

12. **Integrated programs**—*Our programs of theological education must combine spiritual and practical with academic objectives in one holistic integrated educational approach.*

Do theological schools in your region already demonstrate this quality to a high degree?

None do   All do

1   2   3   4   5   6   7

What priority would you assign to efforts to change this aspect of theological education within your region?

No Priority   Highest Priority

1   2   3   4   5   6   7

13. **Servant molding**—*Through our programs of theological education students must be molded to styles of leadership appropriate to their intended biblical role within the body of Christ.*

Do theological schools in your region already demonstrate this quality to a high degree?

None do   All do

1   2   3   4   5   6   7

What priority would you assign to efforts to change this aspect of theological education within your region?

No Priority   Highest Priority

1   2   3   4   5   6   7

14. **Instructional variety**—*Our programs of theological education must vigorously pursue the use of a variety of educational teaching methods.*

Do theological schools in your region already demonstrate this quality to a high degree?

None do   All do

       1   2   3   4   5   6   7

What priority would you assign to efforts to change this aspect of theological education within your region?

No Priority   Highest Priority

       1   2   3   4   5   6   7

15. **A Christian mind**—*Our programs of theological education need much more effectively to model and inculcate a pattern of holistic thought that is openly and wholesomely Biblical.*

Do theological schools in your region already demonstrate this quality to a high degree?

None do   All do

       1   2   3   4   5   6   7

What priority would you assign to efforts to change this aspect of theological education within your region?

No Priority   Highest Priority

       1   2   3   4   5   6   7

16. **Equipping for growth**—*Our programs of theological education need urgently to refocus their patterns of training toward encouraging and facilitating self-directed learning.*

Do theological schools in your region already demonstrate this quality to a high degree?

None do   All do

         1   2   3   4   5   6   7

What priority would you assign to efforts to change this aspect of theological education within your region?

No Priority   Highest Priority

         1   2   3   4   5   6   7

17. **Cooperation**—*Our programs of theological education must pursue contact and collaboration with other evangelical ministry training institutions.*

Do theological schools in your region already demonstrate this quality to a high degree?

None do   All do

         1   2   3   4   5   6   7

What priority would you assign to efforts to change this aspect of theological education within your region?

No Priority   Highest Priority

         1   2   3   4   5   6   7

The twelve points of the ICAA "Manifesto's" agenda for renewal of theological education are listed below.

a. Contextualization	g. Integrated program
b. Churchward orientation	h. Servant molding
c. Strategic flexibility	i. Instructional variety
d. Theological grounding	j. A Christian mind
e. Continuous assessment	k. Equipping for growth
f. Community life	l. Cooperation

18. Please draw a circle around the letter in front of those points which offer the best prospects for **immediate impact** on theological education.

19. Please draw a square around the letter in front of those points which are most important for **long-term renewal** of theological eduction.

20. ICAA adopted the "Manifesto" in its meeting held in June, 1983. Since its adoption, has your agency made use of the "Manifesto" to promote renewal of theological education?

   A.   No
   B.   Yes   [Please list specific uses, including dates and activity or media, on the back of this page.]

21. Within the past 5 years, has your agency attempted to promote among your member institutions any of the commitments or tasks included in the "Manifesto's" agenda (even if the "Manifesto" itself may not have been part of this process)?

   A.   No
   B.   Yes   [Please provide a list of activities aimed at promoting one or more of these values, with date(s) and the specific commitments or tasks focused.]

22. If your agency has attempted to promote renewal values, was the ICAA "Manifesto" a significant stimulus toward developing these activities?

       A.   No—we would probably have done the same things anyway.

       B.   Yes—program development and/or timing was influenced by the "Manifesto."

23. Do you currently have plans to make **new** use of the "Manifesto" within your agency or among your member institutions?

       A.   No

       B.   Yes   [Please describe briefly the plans being made, and give dates of anticipated implementation.]

24. Can you identify any institutions affiliated with your agency which have made significant progress toward renewal of their training programs in any of the areas included in the "Manifesto's" agenda for renewal?

       A.   No

       B.   Yes   [Please provide the following information for each institution (maximum of four):

                      a. Name of institution;
                      b. City where located;
                      c. Specific renewal value(s) observed;
                      d. Factors contributing to observed progress in each area (if known).]

25. Do you know of any other evangelical theological education insti-
    tutions in your international region which have made significant
    progress toward renewal, even though they are not affiliated with
    your agency?

                    A.   No
                    B.   Yes   [Please provide:

                                 a. Name of institution;
                                 b. Name and title of contact person;
                                 c. Mailing address;
                                 d. Telephone number;
                                 e. Specific renewal value(s) observed;
                                 f. Factors contributing to observed progress in
                                    each area (if known).]

26. The purpose of this questionnaire is to understand your priorities
    with respect to renewal of theological education, to determine
    how the ICAA "Manifesto" has been and is being used in your
    agency, and to identify theological education institutions which
    have made significant progress toward renewal of their training
    programs. In light of these purposes, is there anything else that
    you would like to share?

    _____

    _____

    _____

    _____

    _____

27.   The person responsible for the responses on this questionnaire is:

Name _____

Title _____

Telephone _____
            Please include country and/or area code

Please mail this questionnaire to: Dr. Robert Ferris

                    The Billy Graham Center
                    Wheaton College
                    Wheaton, Illinois
                    U. S. A.   60187

Thank you for your assistance. I look forward to sharing with you the findings of this study.

                    Robert Ferris

Questionnaire for ICAA Affiliated Schools

For several years, professional literature on theological education has carried articles discussing the effectiveness of current models of ministry training and calling for reform or renewal of theological education.

1. Do you agree that there is need for renewal of evangelical theological education?

    Strongly Disagree   Strongly Agree

        1   2   3   4   5   6   7

2. If you agree there is need for renewal of theological education, what specifically do you intend to affirm? What changes do you feel are needed to renew theological education?

    _____

    _____

3.   Do you believe substantial change is needed in our approach to
      training for ministry, or do you feel the present approach is serving
      us well?

      Present Approach   Change Is
      Serves Well   Needed

            1   2   3   4   5   6   7

4.   How have you and your faculty attempted to address any need for
      renewal of theological education in your institution?

      _____

      _____

5.   Are you satisfied with the results of these efforts to date?

      Totally   Totally
      Dissatisfied   Satisfied

            1   2   3   4   5   6   7

*There is a notable similarity of concerns among those who advocate renewal of
theological education. This section presents twelve ideals commonly found in
the literature, each followed by four questions.*

6.   **Cultural Appropriateness**—*Training is relevant to traditions, condi-
      tions, and needs in the local society, and is responsive to shifts in social
      norms and values.*

      Is this quality important to you?
                                                    Extremely
          Unimportant   Important

            1   2   3   4   5   6   7

Does your institution already demonstrate this quality?

Not   Thoroughly
Demonstrated   Demonstrated

    1   2   3   4   5   6   7

Within the past five years has your faculty deliberately worked on developing this quality in your ministry training?

    ____ No
    ____ Yes   How? _____

Can you identify any other evangelical ministry training institution you feel demonstrates this quality to a high degree?

    ____ No
    ____ Yes   Name _____
                   City _____

7.   **Attentiveness to the Church**—*Basic orientation is toward the constituent church, rather than academia. Input from churchmen is actively sought and is accorded highest priority in development, delivery, and assessment of training programs.*

Is this quality important to you?

                                       Extremely
Unimportant   Important

    1   2   3   4   5   6   7

Does your institution already demonstrate this quality?

Not   Thoroughly
Demonstrated   Demonstrated

    1   2   3   4   5   6   7

Within the past five years has your faculty deliberately worked on developing this quality in your ministry training?

_____ No
_____ Yes   How? _____

Can you identify any other evangelical ministry training institution you feel demonstrates this quality to a high degree?

_____ No
_____ Yes   Name _____
               City _____

8.   **Flexible Strategizing**—*Educators are aware of the broad spectrum of training needs which may exist in the constituent church, sensitive to needs which do exist, and creative in responding to needs with appropriate training programs.*

Is this quality important to you?

                                              Extremely
Unimportant   Important

     1   2   3   4   5   6   7

Does your institution already demonstrate this quality?

Not   Thoroughly
Demonstrated   Demonstrated

     1   2   3   4   5   6   7

Within the past five years has your faculty deliberately worked on developing this quality in your ministry training?

_____ No
_____ Yes   How? _____

Can you identify any other evangelical ministry training institution you feel demonstrates this quality to a high degree?

_____ No
_____ Yes   Name _____
                 City _____

9.   **Theological Grounding**—*The task and guiding values of theological education are derived from and rooted in a Biblical theology of creation, redemption, Church, and ministry.*

Is this quality important to you?

                                        Extremely
Unimportant   Important

        1   2   3   4   5   6   7

Does your institution already demonstrate this quality?

Not   Thoroughly
Demonstrated   Demonstrated

        1   2   3   4   5   6   7

Within the past five years has your faculty deliberately worked on developing this quality in your ministry training?

_____ No
_____ Yes   How? _____

Can you identify any other evangelical ministry training institution you feel demonstrates this quality to a high degree?

_____ No
_____ Yes   Name _____
                 City _____

10. **Outcomes Assessment**—*The value of education is determined by examining alumni performance in ministry (vs. resources and instructional procedures in the training institution).*

Is this quality important to you?

Unimportant   Extremely
                                         Important

    1   2   3   4   5   6   7

Does your institution already demonstrate this quality?

Not   Thoroughly
Demonstrated   Demonstrated

    1   2   3   4   5   6   7

Within the past five years has your faculty deliberately worked on developing this quality in your ministry training?

        ____ No
        ____ Yes   How? _____

Can you identify any other evangelical ministry training institution you feel demonstrates this quality to a high degree?

        ____ No
        ____ Yes   Name _____
                    City _____

11. **Spiritual Formation**—*A community life is cultivated which promotes and facilitates growth in grace.*

Is this quality important to you?

Unimportant   Extremely
                                         Important

    1   2   3   4   5   6   7

Does your institution already demonstrate this quality?

Not   Thoroughly
Demonstrated   Demonstrated

          1   2   3   4   5   6   7

Within the past five years has your faculty deliberately worked on developing this quality in your ministry training?

          ____ No
          ____ Yes   How? _____

Can you identify any other evangelical ministry training institution you feel demonstrates this quality to a high degree?

          ____ No
          ____ Yes   Name _____
                        City _____

12. **Holistic Curricularizing**—*Academic, practical, and spiritual training is integrated into a unified program of professional development.*

Is this quality important to you?

                                                      Extremely
Unimportant   Important

          1   2   3   4   5   6   7

Does your institution already demonstrate this quality?

Not   Thoroughly
Demonstrated   Demonstrated

          1   2   3   4   5   6   7

Within the past five years has your faculty deliberately worked on developing this quality in your ministry training?

_____ No
_____ Yes   How? _____

Can you identify any other evangelical ministry training institution you feel demonstrates this quality to a high degree?

_____ No
_____ Yes   Name _____
              City _____

13. **Service Orientation**—*Emphasis is placed on leadership as servanthood; elitist attitudes are consciously renounced.*

Is this quality important to you?

                                        Extremely
Unimportant   Important

     1   2   3   4   5   6   7

Does your institution already demonstrate this quality?

Not   Thoroughly
Demonstrated   Demonstrated

     1   2   3   4   5   6   7

Within the past five years has your faculty deliberately worked on developing this quality in your ministry training?

_____ No
_____ Yes   How? _____

Can you identify any other evangelical ministry training institution you feel demonstrates this quality to a high degree?

_____ No
_____ Yes   Name _____
              City _____

14. **Creativity in Teaching**—*Teaching methods are selected reflectively or developed creatively to correlate with instructional goals.*

Is this quality important to you?

Unimportant   Extremely
                                               Important

    1   2   3   4   5   6   7

Does your institution already demonstrate this quality?

Not   Thoroughly
Demonstrated   Demonstrated

    1   2   3   4   5   6   7

Within the past five years has your faculty deliberately worked on developing this quality in your ministry training?

    ____ No
    ____ Yes   How? _____

Can you identify any other evangelical ministry training institution you feel demonstrates this quality to a high degree?

    ____ No
    ____ Yes   Name _____
                 City _____

15. **A Christian Worldview**—*Training seeks to cultivate a mindset in which the Bible is the standard for measuring every area of life and thought.*

Is this quality important to you?

Unimportant   Extremely
                                               Important

    1   2   3   4   5   6   7

Does your institution already demonstrate this quality?

Not   Thoroughly
Demonstrated   Demonstrated

    1   2   3   4   5   6   7

Within the past five years has your faculty deliberately worked on developing this quality in your ministry training?

_____ No
_____ Yes   How? _____

Can you identify any other evangelical ministry training institution you feel demonstrates this quality to a high degree?

_____ No
_____ Yes   Name _____
             City _____

16. **A Developmental Focus**—*Faculty-student interactions are deliberately designed to encourage and facilitate self-directed learning; methods cultivating dependencies are resolutely resisted.*

Is this quality important to you?

                                                       Extremely
Unimportant   Important

    1   2   3   4   5   6   7

Does your institution already demonstrate this quality?

Not   Thoroughly
Demonstrated   Demonstrated

    1   2   3   4   5   6   7

Within the past five years has your faculty deliberately worked on developing this quality in your ministry training?

_____ No
_____ Yes   How? _____

Can you identify any other evangelical ministry training institution you feel demonstrates this quality to a high degree?

_____ No
_____ Yes   Name _____
              City _____

17. **A Cooperative Spirit**—*Institutional leadership is committed to open communication and collaboration among evangelical theological education institutions.*

Is this quality important to you?

                                    Extremely
Unimportant   Important

    1   2   3   4   5   6   7

Does your institution already demonstrate this quality?

Not   Thoroughly
Demonstrated   Demonstrated

    1   2   3   4   5   6   7

Within the past five years has your faculty deliberately worked on developing this quality in your institution?

_____ No
_____ Yes   How? _____

Can you identify any other evangelical ministry training institution you feel demonstrates this quality to a high degree?

_____ No

_____ Yes   Name _____

City _____

18. Are you aware of the International Council of Accrediting Agencies for evangelical theological education (I.C.A.A.)?

A. No

B. Somewhat aware

C. Very aware

19. In 1983, I.C.A.A. published a "Manifesto on the Renewal of Evangelical Theological Education." Are you familiar with the basic contents of the I.C.A.A. "Manifesto"?

A. No [Skip to question 21.]

B. Not sure [Skip to question 21.]

C. Yes

20. If you are familiar with the I.C.A.A. "Manifesto," have you used it in any way to promote renewal of theological education in your institution?

A. No.

B. Yes   [A brief explanation of how you have used the "Manifesto," as well as comments about its usefulness, would be very helpful. You may use the back of this sheet.]

21.   Would you like to know more about I.C.A.A. and its efforts to promote renewal of evangelical theological education?

> A. No, thank you.
> B. Yes

22.   The person responsible for the responses on this questionnaire is:

Name _____

Title _____

Institution _____

Address _____

Telephone _____
Please include country and/or area code

Please mail this questionnaire to: Dr. Robert Ferris
                                          Graham Center Administration
                                          Wheaton College
                                          Wheaton, Illinois   60187

Thank you for your assistance. If you desire a summary of the findings of this study, I will be happy to provide one on request.
                                Robert Ferris

Syllabus of Two Year Course*
All Nations Christian College

The course consists of lectures and seminars, some of which are foundational (the 'Core' subjects) while others are more specialist ('Electives'). Students will determine their own study programme in consultation with their tutor. They are normally expected to attend all the lectures and seminars in the Core Course, whereas attendance at the 'Electives' is optional and will be determined by the specialist interests of the individual student.

In addition to the following, one complete week in each year is devoted to integrated studies in one O.T. or N.T. book.

The College may change some courses from time to time in response to staff changes and in order to meet new needs.

First Year

Biblical Studies

Core Subjects:
O.T. *Background:* The historical background; the literature; the key theological themes of the O.T.
O.T. *Exposition:* Genesis - Deuteronomy.
N.T. *Background:* The ministry of Jesus; the faith and activity of the early church in its historical context.
N.T. *Exposition:* Romans 1 - 13; 1 Corinthians.

* From the College *Prospectus* current in 1989

Electives:
O.T. Exposition: Jonah.
N.T. Exposition: Mark; Luke; 1 Thessalonians.
Greek: An introduction to the grammar and syntax of N.T. Greek.

Historical and Theological Studies

Core Subjects:
Early Church History: To 451 AD.
Hermeneutics: The principles and practice of biblical interpretation.
Doctrine of the Church: Its life, work, ministry, ordinances and mission.

Elective:
Apologetics: An examination of the Christian world view, as it relates to the communication of the gospel to a secular, pluralistic world.

Missiological Studies

Core Subjects:
Biblical Basis of Mission: A study of God's purposes for the nations in the Old and New Testaments.
History of Christian Mission: A study of the expansion of the church, and its application to mission today.
Understanding Culture: Culture—its importance and influence on people and the communication process and anthropology.
Missionary Methods in Practice: A study of practical aspects of the work of mission, e.g. lay training, pioneer evangelism, church structures, etc.
Wholistic Mission: Evangelism and social transformation; theology of development; social justice.
Church Growth: Principles and practice.
Introduction to World Religions: Beliefs and practices of Primal Religions, Eastern Religions, Islam and Judaism.
Marxism: Background influences on Marx, key elements of his thought, a Christian critique.
Roman Catholicism: Trent, Vatican I and II and the changes today.
Christianity in Today's World: The practical application of the principles of Christian mission in today's changing world.

Electives:
Orthodox Christianity: Theology and practice of Eastern Orthodox churches.
Medical Missions: Community health, strategies and policies for medical mission.
Introduction to Linguistics: Basic studies in phonetics, structure of language and language learning.
Student Ministry: The importance, potential and principles of outreach to students.
Prejudice, Discrimination and Racism: The origins and impact of prejudice.
Post-Marx Marxism: Lenin, Mao, Marxist views of religion, Eurocommunism.

Pastoral Studies

Core Subjects:
Pastoral Studies: Basic understanding of personhood and of the principles of pastoral care and counselling; patterns of reaction; stress; dynamics of relationships.
Cross-Cultural Life and Work: Issues relating to the daily missionary life.
Spiritual Warfare and Deliverance Ministry: Biblical teaching and current cross-cultural experience.
Communicating the Gospel: Christian education for all ages and cultures; practical training in speaking, evangelism, conduct of worship; introduction to and use of modern media.

Elective:
Pastoral Studies: Enrichment seminars for single, engaged and married students.

Second Year

Biblical Studies

Core Subjects:
O.T. Exposition: Isaiah 1 - 12; Haggai, Zechariah, Malachi.
N.T. Exposition: Christological passages; Ephesians; Gospel of John.

Electives:

O.T. Exposition: Psalms and Wisdom Literature.

N.T. Exposition: Matthew; Revelation.

Greek: A study of selected passages from the Greek N.T. A continuation of First Year course.

Hebrew: An introduction to the grammar and syntax of biblical Hebrew.

Historical and Theological Studies

Core Subjects:

Doctrines of God, Person and Work of Christ, The Holy Spirit: Studies in the doctrine of humanity and ethics.

Doctrine of the Last Things: Perspectives on events before and after the parousia. Views on the millennium.

Church History: Developments in Europe since the Reformation.

Missiological Studies

Core Subjects:

History of Christian Mission: A continuation of First Year course.

Theology of Mission: Studies of issues in current debate and a survey and appraisal of key missiological statements in Evangelical, Ecumenical and Roman Catholic circles.

Gospel and Culture: Making the gospel culturally relevant; the influence of the gospel on culture.

Cross-Cultural Life and Work: Practical issues relating to the daily life of a missionary. A continuation of First Year course.

Current Missiological Issues: Group discussion on questions relating to missionary life and practice.

Christianity in Today's World: A continuation of First Year course.

Leadership and Management in Christian Organisations:

Electives:

Specialist Studies in Religions: Traditional Religion, Buddhism, Hinduism, Chinese and Japanese Religions, Judaism, Islam.

Non-European Theological Developments: Contextualisation; Latin American, African, Indian and East Asian contributions to theological thinking.

New Religious Movements: Beliefs of, and Christian approach to, sects and cults.

Independency Churches: Reasons for growth, characteristics of and new approaches to.

Anglicanism: Its history, principles and practices.

Urban Mission: Urbanisation, the city in the Bible, strategies to reach cities, plus observation visits.

Theological Education by Extension: Its history, principles and practice.

Pastoral Studies

Core Subjects:

Pastoral Studies: Dynamics of loss and change. A continuation of First Year course.

Communicating the Gospel: Workshops in exegetical and expository skills. A continuation of First Year course.

Placement Debriefing: Debriefing following students' residential block placement.

Electives:

Bible Meditation: Study and practice of the principles of Bible meditation.

Pastoral Studies: Elective seminars developing further pastoral skills. A continuation of First Year course.

SELECTED STUDY ASSIGNMENTS*
All Nations Christian College

New Testament Background (Year 1, Term 1) Two units if both parts are attempted.

   Part I   Study the text of the Acts of the Apostles.

   a) Write a brief summary (500-1000 words) of the main stages in the spread of the gospel, noting obstacles encountered and how they were overcome.
   b) Make a comparison of the form and content of the sermons in Acts. Are the similarities and differences related to the varying audiences?

   Reading—
Acts	I H Marshall
Evangelism in the Early Church	E M B Green
Evangelism—Now and Then	E M B Green
The Apostolic Age	G B Caird

   Part II   From your study of Acts and referring to:

   Missionary Methods: St Paul's or Ours R Allen

   Write briefly on the following question:

   How far can we make Paul's methods a pattern for missionary work today?

---

* Taken from "Study Assignments" sheets for 1988/89

Biblical Basis of Mission (Year 1, Term 1) One unit.

Read: The Biblical Foundations for Mission
       Senior & Stuhlmueller

Write a talk or sermon for a missionary meeting, using Ephesians or Colossians as your text.

Or:

What, in your understanding, is the relationship between the Kingdom of God and mission?

Books for Reference—
Mission Between the Times	C R Padilla
Discipling the Nations	R R de Ridder
Contemporary Theologies of Mission	A Glasser
God's Mission: Healing the Nations	D Burnett
The Kingdom of God	J Bright
God's Kingdom for Today	P Toon
The Open Secret	L Newbigin
The Biblical Foundations for Mission	Senior & Stuhlmueller

Doctrine of the Church (Year 1, Term 2) One unit.

Read: Know the Truth by B Milne, part 6.

Also write on one of the following:

a) What is the place and meaning of baptism and/or communion in Christian worship?
b) What is the nature of the offices apostle, bishop/elder, deacon in the New Testament? Is there any evidence for the continuation of these ministries in the present day?

Reading —

a) The Water that Divides	D Bridge & D Phypers
Baptism in the NT	G Beasley-Murray
Last Supper, Lord's Supper	I H Marshall

b) Cinderella with Amnesia   M Griffiths
   Freed to Serve   M Green
   Let My People Grow   M Harper

See also in general:
   Christian Theology, Vol 3   M Erickson
   I Believe in the Church   D Watson
   Articles in Bible and Theological dictionaries.

Pastoral Studies (Year 1, Term 2) One unit.

Discuss the possible links between your experience of your primary family and your own patterns of relationship and reaction now.

Make reference to:
   Lectures on Pastoral Studies
   Lecture notes "Understanding Culture"
   Overcoming Hurts and Anger   Carlson
   Conflict: Friend or Foe   Huggett
   Christian Counselling   G Collins

Gospel and Culture (Year 2, Term 2)

Write on one of the following:

a) With reference to OT and NT describe and attempt to evaluate the variety of relationships between God's covenant people and the surrounding culture.

   Living as the People of God   C J H Wright
   Down to Earth   Scott & Cooke

b) Read Christ and Culture (H R Niebuhr). In the light of Niebuhr's book, describe and evaluate the relationship between the Church and culture in any society known to you.

Union Biblical Seminary, Pune
Bachelor of Divinity Course Offerings

			Total No Of Classes	Credit For The Course
First Year (Including Orientation Session)				
GE	1	English and Study Skills	50	Full Course
Bib	1	Bible Survey and Background	50	Full Course
OT	1	Pentateuch (Intro, Contents, Theology)	30	Half Course
NT	1	Life and Teachings of Jesus (Synoptics)	30	Half Course
TH	1	Outlines of Christian Theology	50	Full Course
CH	1	Intro to History of Christianity	50	Full Course
CM	1	Leadership in the Local Church	60*	Full Course
CM	2	Principles of Preaching and Teaching	60*	Full Course
CM	3	Principles of Pastoral Care & Counselling	60*	Full Course
TE	1	Missions: Bib'l, Theo'l & Contemp. Trends	50	Full Course
		Introduction to Biblical Languages	10	
Plus		One Biblical language, either/or		
OT	4	Hebrew Grammar	90	Full Course
NT	4	Greek Grammar	90	Full Course
And		The second Bib'l lang OR 2 Electives	1 1/2	Full Courses

* Includes ten hours for micro-teaching/practice.

Second Year (In Internship)

TH	3	Church & Christian Ethics in Contemp Soc.	50	Full Course
RS	1	Religions in India	50	Full Course
CH	2	History of Christianity in India	50 (S)	Full Course
OT	2	Prophets (Intro, Contents, Theology)	50 (S)	Full Course

Third Year

Bib	2	Biblical Interpretation and Criticism	50		Full Course
Bib	3	Biblical Theology	30		Half Course
OT	3	Psalms and Wisdom (Intro, Cont, Theo)	30		Half Course
NT	2	Pauline Thought	50 (S)		Full Course
NT	3	John and Johannine Thought	30		Half Course
TH	2	Indian Christian Theology	50 (S)		Full Course
RS	2	MRSM since 1947	50 (S)		Full Course
Plus:		2 Electives		2	Full Courses
And:		A Thesis (or 2 additional Electives)		1 1/2	Full Courses
		TOTAL		24 1/2	Full Courses

Purpose of the Internship Year*
Union Biblical Seminary

Training for ministry can ultimately only be given by actual involvement in ministry. The best place for this is in the context of a "live" situation, with adequate time for *exposure* and *involvement* as well as *reflection* on the experience. We have tried several ways to do this. Our coming to Pune has resulted in a dramatic increase in opportunities and in the quality of practical training. But we still feel that this can only be done adequately by a longer period [of involvement in ministry]. We also feel that it is vitally important for us to enter into much closer and more active partnership with our sponsoring churches, so that we can make use of the resources available off campus.

So the purpose [of the internship year] is to help the students:

(a)   to understand the nature of the church and its mission in the world through the experience of involvement in a local church (or other community) in its context in society;

(b)   to develop skills in areas of ministry, including administration, worship, preaching and teaching, relating to people, equipping people for ministry, evangelism, and social involvement;

(c)   to reflect on ministry from theological, ethical, historical, and social perspectives, by studying related courses; and

(d)   to plan and use time in such a way as to balance the demands of ministry, study and reflection, and personal growth.

* From a mimeographed document titled, "The Internship Year: Preliminary Information" (Union Biblical Seminary, Pune. n.d.).

Guidelines for Using Case Studies in Teaching and Learning*
Union Biblical Seminary

A. Introduction

One of the most important ways in which we learn is from personal experience. Such learning helps to integrate head and heart, activity and reflection, the academic and the spiritual. But in order to learn from our experience we need to know how to analyse it and reflect on it.

There are four steps in this process:

1. Experiencing: There must be a direct experience of some event or activity.

2. Analysing : What were the factors in the experience—cause, background, underlying issues, etc. Why did it happen as it did?

3. Generalising: What principles can be learned from this analysis?

4. Theologising: What is a Christian and Biblical understanding of this experience and the principles derived from it?

---

* A mimeographed paper by this title (Union Biblical Seminary, Pune, n.d.), developed from Mulholland, K. and Lores, R., "Case Study Methodology," in *Extension Seminary*, No. 3, 1977, pp. 1-9.

We can, and should, engage in this kind of critical reflection on our own. But we can also do a great deal to help each other in this process, with mutual benefit. This especially applies in a small group situation.

One method which can be most effectively used here is through *case studies.*

A *case* is a description of an act or event in which (usually) the writer has been involved and for which he bears some responsibility for the outcome.

This description is presented to a group or class, who then reflect together on it in order to *learn* from the experience and from each other, to help each other to develop understanding and skills for more effective ministry. (This method can be used in any educational field).

Through the group process the writer is helped to discover more from his own experience, and the group is helped to enter into his experience and learn from it. Dimensions which had not been explored are often brought to light.

B. Prepare the Case

The complexity of the case will determine [the length of] the description, from a minimum of five typewritten single spaced pages. Part of the discipline is to learn to condense, utilizing only the most important information. It is recommended that one begin with less complicated cases and advance progressively to more complicated ones as he masters the method. Sometimes one can utilize only a single episode or isolated incident that can be described in one or two paragraphs followed by some questions in regard to the attitude and activity of the persons involved in the incident, and the criteria and principles that enter the picture.

There are five distinct parts that the writer has to describe clearly:

A. Background. It is necessary to provide sufficient information to place the case in its context, especially the historical background of the persons or institutions that are involved in the case. Such currents of ideological opinion, tradition, events, etc. that determine or affect the case, ought to be pointed out.

B.   Description. What happened? How? When? Include as many important details as possible. You can use direct quotes including, for instance, a conversation or dialogue.

C.   Analysis. Identify the important factors that intervene. Take into account the interpersonal dynamic, with special attention to changes of attitude, behavior, etc. In problems of change or innovation, analyse the process. Add the implications of the event and the situation that has resulted as a consequence of the same.

D.   Solution. Here one indicates clearly but concisely the decision that was taken and the reasons or bases that brought it about. The writer can place before the group a question that he may have in regard to his own activity, in order that he may receive the help of the group. One educational mode is to state here only various possible alternatives to the solution of the case and to allow the group to come up with a solution. After a time of discussion the writer presents the solution that the case had in reality and discusses and compares it with the proposals of the group.

E.   Evaluation. If you desire, you can include an evaluation of your own action, indicating whether you believe that you reached your objective.

C. Discussing the Case

The group can vary in number from five to twelve persons. There should be a leader or "facilitator" who convenes the group, maintains the time table, and keeps the discussion moving. It is also good to assign one or two "evaluators" who study the case beforehand and prepare a written evaluation. If possible, the writer should also distribute copies of the case to all the groups beforehand.
N.B. The case *must* be written. This provides a discipline for the writer to express himself concisely, clearly, and comprehensively.

The meeting should follow a fairly strict schedule.

1.   *Presentation* (if the case has not been previously circulated).

2. *Questions for clarification*—These are only to clarify what is written, not to add new information or to begin the analysis.

3. *Analysis of the event*—What are the underlying issues, causes, factors? Why did things happen as they did? What are the motives of the people involved? If no solution has been indicated, what are the possible solutions?

4. *Evaluation of the solution*—This has two parts: (a) evaluation of the event and its solution or possible solutions, from a biblical, theological, historical perspective. Relevant Biblical passages may be used here; and (b) evaluation of the writer's competence, both in preparing the case and in his actual involvement.

5. *Response and reflection*—The writer is not allowed to speak during the previous two parts. This can be frustrating! Now he is asked for his reactions (a) to the experience itself, and (b) to the discussion. This is important, since our *feelings* reflect our personal involvement (as distinct from our ideas and opinions). From such sharing, deep mutual understanding can come.

6. *Prayer*—For those involved in the experience, and for the new lessons and insights learned.

Servant-Leaders for the Church in India*
Union Biblical Seminary

Purpose

The purpose of the Seminary, as described in the Constitution, is to enable people to become servant-leaders for the varied ministries of the Church in India.

Objectives

A. Recognizing the Biblical variety of ministries and the different calling of each person, our objective is to train those who will exercise the following ministries:

1) Bible exposition, teaching, and training
2) Evangelism and church planting, both locally and cross-culturally
3) Exercising pastoral care and concern
4) Leadership in the life and activities of the congregation (worship, instruction, fellowship, and outreach)
5) Active involvement in meeting the needs of India (especially bearing in mind the needs of the poor and oppressed and those in rural areas and the pluralism of religious and political ideologies.)

B. The *goal* of all these ministries, in accordance with the Biblical pattern, is to motivate and equip all members of the church/congregation for the ministry which God has given them.

* A mimeographed paper by this title (Pune: Union Biblical Seminary, n.d.).

C. The *focus* of all these ministries is to serve and build the local church, since it is the key to mission and evangelization in God's plan.

D. The *personal qualities* needed to fulfill these ministries will include:

1) secure and growing commitment to God
2) understanding and acceptance of themselves
3) a sense of commitment to the church, the fellowship of God's people
4) a sense of calling and recognition by others of gifts for ministry (Eph 4:11, ff.)
5) ability to relate to others with love and concern
6) obedience to the Word of God in thinking and practice
7) ability to fulfill their responsibility to their families

In order to fulfill these above objectives, the following specific objectives will be needed:

Objectives arising out of the general objectives (a tentative list)

A. *Ministries*

1) *Bible exposition, teaching, and training*

Knowledge - of the Bible: content, structure, overall message, details of books, etc.
- of the principles of preaching, teaching, communication

Attitudes - commitment to the importance of Bible expository and teaching ministry for building the church

Skills - ability to expound a passage relevantly in different situations, for large or small groups
- ability to prepare for exposition by careful exegesis, inductive study, etc.
- ability to use tools for study

2) *Evangelism and church planting*

    Knowledge - the message of the gospel
                    - the mission of the church
                    - the culture, religions, and ideologies of the people evangelised
                    - bridges for the gospel into the particular culture

    Attitudes - passion for evangelism
                    - identification with people

    Skills   - able to use different methods of evangelism according to the situation
                    - able to establish and build a church in a new situation

3) *Pastoral care and concern*

    Knowledge - different types of people
                    - principles of counselling

    Attitudes - concern and respect for people as individuals and for the whole person
    Skills   - able to listen, discern, ask questions
                    - able to relate Biblical principles to people's needs

4) *Leadership in the life of the congregation*

    Knowledge - the functions of the church
                    - the role different members can play
                    - principles of leadership and management

    Attitudes - commitment to the building of the church
                    - concern to develop members' gifts
                    - willing to take risks and responsibilities of leadership without power and domination

    Skills   - able to plan, organise, lead, and control

effectively
- able to manage his own time

5) *Active involvement in meeting needs*

Knowledge - the church and its mission in the context
- society and culture and the needs
- Biblical principles relevant to the needs

Attitudes - concern and respect for people in their totality
- commitment to the development of healthy, just society
- willingness to sacrifice

Skills - able to motivate people for change
- able to use the dynamics of change in a society
- able to help people practically

B. *The Goal: Motivating and Equipping*

Knowledge - the biblical pattern of ministry, especially the function of all members in the body
- present misconceptions of pastor-centered ministry
- cultural factors in the concept of leadership
- principles of teaching and training

Attitudes - commitment to building the body and developing members' gifts
- willingness to be a member of a team
- sharing leadership and responsibility
- building on his strengths, recognising his weaknesses
- invaling [sic] others in ministry
- willingness to learn from others
- willingness to be flexible and mobile if necessary

Skills - able to motivate, encourage, and develop others
- able to communicate and pass on what he has learned

- able to understand and make use of the
  dynamics of change
- able to train others for leadership

C. *Focus on Local Church*

Knowledge - the doctrine of the church and especially the
              place of the local church in God's plan

Attitudes - faith in God's purpose and will to work
              through his church
           - commitment to serve and build the local
              church despite problems
           - commitment to active membership of a
              particular local church, wherever one is

Skills   - able to relate his ministry to the local church
              and to enter into its life

D. *Personal Qualities*

1) *Secure and growing commitment to God*

Knowledge - God and his place in God's plan
           - assurance of God's love on the basis of the
              work of Christ

Attitudes - God-consciousness
           - love for God and desire to serve Him

Skills   - able to use regularly the means of grace
              (prayer, Bible, worship, fellowship) despite
              pressure
           - able to face crises such as doubt or external
              pressure

2) *Understanding and acceptance of himself*

Knowledge - Biblical understanding of himself in God's
              plan
           - principles of psychology and counselling

Attitudes   - sense of humour

Skills   - able to recognise his strengths and weaknesses
                and correct or build on them

3) *Commitment to the church, the fellowship of God's people*

Knowledge   - the doctrine of the church and its relevance

Attitudes   - commitment to the churches, God's agent in
               the world
            - willingness to see himself as a member of the
               congregation, with the same rights and
               responsibilities as others
            - commitment to sharing with others on a
               regular basis
            - willingness to receive pastoral care and
               concern from others
Skills   - able to share with others on a regular basis

4) *Sense of calling and recognition by others of gifts for ministry*

Knowledge   - Biblical principles of gifts, calling, ministry
            - knowledge of his own gifts, on the basis of
               recognition by others, prayer, etc.

Attitudes   - willingness to obey God's calling
            - willing to develop his gifts and use them for
               others
            - willing to serve others through his ministry

Skills   - able to discover and develop his own gifts
            - able to discover God's guidance

5) *Ability to relate to others with love and concern*

Knowledge   - Biblical principles and examples

Attitudes   - willing to learn from others
            - willing to accept all kinds of people
            - love for persons as individuals and for the
               whole of man

Skills   -   [No entry provided.]

6) *Obedience to the Word of God in thinking and practice*

Knowledge -   main principles of Biblical/Theological
                   disciplines, their relationship to each other,
                   and their relevance and application to his life
                   and ministry
               -   relationship of these principles to other
                   disciplines
               -   other ideologies and world views, and their
                   relationship to the Biblical world view

Attitudes   -   willing to apply the Word of God to all aspects
                   of life and obey it, as an individual and as a
                   member of society
               -   willing to discipline himself and grow in body,
                   mind, and spirit
               -   willing to go on studying to develop himself
                   and his ministry

Skills   -   able to keep himself fit, mentally, physically,
                   spiritually
               -   able to judge all issues from a Biblical
                   perspective
               -   able to think critically and creatively and to
                   form judgments

7) *Ability to fulfill responsibility to their families*

Knowledge -   Biblical principles of the family and their
                   relationship to his culture
               -   roles of different members of the family and
                   their responsibilities

Attitudes   -   [No entry provided.]

Skills   -   able to balance other roles with family role

Excerpts From an Unpublished Paper

How to Strengthen Our Training:
A Proposal for Integrating Supervised Field Experience
(Ministry and Study) into Our Curriculum

By Robin Thomson
Union Biblical Seminary
Pune, 1986

Summary

The essence of this proposal is that we restructure our whole training programme into three major blocks:

(a) An initial period on-campus of three to three and a half terms*;

(b) A central period off-campus of eighteen to twenty-four months, in which a student would be engaged in supervised ministry and study in a local situation (or more than one place);

(c) A final period on campus of three to three and a half terms.

It can immediately be seen that this is in some ways a radical proposal (in other ways it is quite conservative). It combines different methods of training, in an attempt to get the best out of them and provide a more effective approach than our present one.

* At the time Thomson wrote, UBS was on a calendar which provided three eleven-week terms per academic year.

Basis

The basis for this proposal is given quite briefly here. I have discussed some of the underlying presuppositions in an earlier paper "The Crisis of Training for Ministry," presented to the Society for Biblical Studies in December 1982.

1. All the evidence of educators, both Christian and secular, points to the indispensable role of supervised experience in any kind of *training* for professional roles (medical, teaching, scientific, pastoral, etc.). While this experience could come at the end of the period of theoretical study, or be incorporated as part of the weekly routine, there is increasing evidence of the value of blocks of time for field experience, with the opportunity for later theoretical study and reflection on the experiences. (See Brian Hill's paper to the Faculty—January 1984—"Theological Education: Is It Out of Practice?")

2. Along with this is the evidence from our own UBS experience of the alienation from their context which many of our students undergo because of their three or more years on campus. Weekend ministry has a vital place in preventing or correcting this, but even in the Pune-Bombay region our present curriculum structure does not permit us to take full advantage of this. Our present summer ministry periods are also *very* uneven in their value.

3. At present we face serious difficulties in motivating the majority of our students *either* for ministry *or* for creative and critical academic study and reflection. This is because, with a few exceptions, students are limited by:

    (a) their previous academic background with rote-learning emphasis;
    (b) their lack of experience of life and ministry;
    (c) our inability to help them to learn to study and think because of our present teaching methods and large classes.

    There are exceptions to this, but we must be concerned for the *majority* of students, for whom this is true. These gaps can only be filled, as I see it, by direct field experience.

4. There are rich resources of learning experiences available in churches and other agencies that are involved in ministry, some in "frontier" situations, which we need to make use of in providing a curriculum for our students. We need to develop a "network" with these. We cannot provide all the experiences necessary, or available, with our limited resources.

5. Following on from this, we need to link our training much more closely with the sending churches. In March 1985 several requests were made by participants in the Consultation for UBS to add certain ingredients to the training. Some of these are *beyond* our resources. In fact, the churches can provide several areas of training much more effectively than we can. For example, development of the regional languages, or familiarity with local church or denominational beliefs and practices. There are many more areas like these. We need to enter into partnership with sending churches, which will result in a much more effective training.

6. This approach will combine and synthesize the strengths of both extension and residential approaches to training, while minimising the weaknesses of both. In fact, many students are looking for this kind of synthesis as a creative alternative to *either* residential *or* extension training.

7. This proposal should result in strengthening of *all three* components of our training—academic, spiritual, and practical.

Proposal Summary

That we divide our training into three major blocks, as follows:

(a) Initial Period on Campus—3 or 3 1/2 terms

    Emphasis: learning how to study
               introduction to basic disciplines, languages, etc.
               involvement in ministry in the local church
               exposure to social and cultural context
               personal growth and group/community life

(b) Field Experience—1 1/2 or 2 years

    Emphasis: involvement in ministry, under supervision
                  on-going study (1/3 of total subjects)
                  reflection on their ministry and context

(c) Final Period on Campus—3 or 3 1/2 terms

    Emphasis: reflection on their ministry and context
                  study with an emphasis on inter-disciplinary and inte-
                  grative approach
                  involvement in ministry

. . . . .

Conclusion

The above is only an outline proposal. Many more details need to be filled in. We need to consider the best way to go forward and then take it.

Are there any alternatives?

1. *The present system continued.* The status quo always seems to be safer, but in our present situation I doubt whether many will argue for it.

2. *Shorter periods off campus—up to six months.* This may *appear* to be less disrupting, but it would be much more difficult to become really involved or useful in such a comparatively short period of time. So it would be hard to arrange for proper supervision and to combine it with study. I do not think it would prove to be much better than our present summer break period. Of course, the B.Th. students until recently had this five month break and so we can discuss and learn from their experience. I did not observe any significant impact of the five month break period. Some had a seventeen month break. On the other hand, even those with a longer break still had to complete the same number of years on campus. It was still a "break." The new proposal is not for a "break," but for combining two different, complementary approaches to study.

3. *One year at the end, between completing studies and receiving the diploma.* In this pattern (which is used by [Union Theological College, Bangalore,] and perhaps other colleges), students have to complete one year of ministry after leaving the college. Then they return for a week or so of reflection and *then* they get their diploma.

    This is no doubt valuable, and relatively easy to implement (though some still think it is a radical idea!). But the college would have relatively little or no control over that year. It might or might not prove to be a training experience (though it probably would). Also, there would be little opportunity for the student to reflect on his experience and then direct his further studies in the light of that experience.

4. *Radical restructuring of the weekly schedule on campus, in order to provide rich and varied field experience in the Pune-Bombay area.* This would be a very valuable alternative. In fact, it probably should be done in any case. The problem would be to provide adequate supervision for the *large* numbers of our students involved. Even with our present fairly minimal practical training, there is a problem of supervision. All faculty members do not have the same amount of time, experience, or gifts. Such a programme would almost certainly mean that *all* faculty members would have to take part, about two days a week, or the equivalent.

    This still remains a viable alternative, however, to the main proposal. In my opinion, it would be harder and more demanding to implement. And it would be quite difficult to adjust to a weekly rhythm of, say, two days' practical work and four days' study (or various combinations or permutations of that). Also, exams, vacations, etc., tend to disrupt such practical work.

In my opinion, the original proposal remains the best alternative. But that is now for all of us to decide!

APPENDIX K

TRAINING GOALS
Conservative Baptist Seminary of the East

Ministry Skills to be Developed by Pastoral Trainees

Preaching—Students will be able to preach effective and interesting expository sermons.

Teaching—Students will be able to teach biblical materials to all age groups using adult learning principles.

Ceremonies—Students will be able to conduct the ceremonies of their receiving churches such as baptism, the Lord's Supper, Christian funerals, weddings, and the dedication of infants.

Worship Services—Students will be able to plan and conduct dynamic, Christ-centered worship services.

Pastoral Care—

Students will be able to minister to the sick.
Students will be able to give competent pastoral counseling within the context of the local church.

Missions and Evangelism—

Students will be able to restore inactive members and incorporate
    transfer members into the local church.
Students will acquire an ability to aid the needy through social services
    and participation in community activities.
Because the making of Christian disciples is the main purpose of the
    church, students will be able to disciple others singly and in
    groups.
Students will participate significantly in some phase of starting a new
    church.
Students will learn to minister to ethnics who have not been assimilated
    into American mainstream culture.
Students will be able to plan a local church mission program.

Management and Leadership—

Recognizing that working cooperatively is essential to effective Chris-
    tian ministry, students will learn how to get along with and to lead
    others.
Students will develop skills of effective church management.
Students will be able to initiate, develop, lead, and deploy small groups
    in the local church for the purposes of evangelism, discipleship,
    prayer, and fellowship.

Character Traits Appropriate to a Pastoral Trainee

Students will possess good reputations and clear consciences. Some of
    the attitudes and actions appropriate to this objective are:

    1. Stability
    2. Consistency
    3. Confidence
    4. Being above reproach
    5. Having a good reputation and testimony among Christians and
       non-Christians

Students will be devoted to the attitudes and disciplines of a godly life.
    Some of the attitudes and actions appropriate to this objective are:

1. A walk of faith
2. Consistent striving for spiritual growth
3. Acceptance of suffering and conflict as part of spiritual growth
4. Freedom from fear
5. Spiritual and moral discernment
6. Freedom to surrender personal rights for Christ's sake (1 Cor. 9)
7. Moral and ethical thought and action
8. Effective prayer and devotional life
9. Humility
10. Prudence; making wise decisions
11. Clear and God-centered self-identity
12. Thinking and praying to arrive at conclusions; not impulsive
13. Open to correction; teachable

Students will demonstrate pleasing social qualities and skills. Some of the attitudes and actions appropriate to this objective are:

1. Honesty before God and genuineness before others; sincerity
2. Practice of Christian tolerance (Romans 14)
3. Correct response to criticism and new ideas
4. Kind and even-tempered
5. Able to discuss issues with moderation and insight; non-threatened
6 Compatible; works well with a wide variety of persons
7. Cares for personal appearance; decorous
8. Gentle and merciful to others
9. Hospitable

Students will be dedicated to healthy family life and friendships. Some of the attitudes and actions appropriate to this objective are:

1. Meeting family responsibilities
2. Managing well their own homes
3. Being loyal, faithful
4. Continually learning and growing in skills and attitudes regarding marriage and parenting
5. Choosing friends wisely
6. Having children who are well-behaved and followers of Christ

Students will show self-control in areas of sexuality, money, use of
authority,time and appetites. Some of the attitudes and actions
appropriate to this objective are:

1. Biblical stewardship of time, money, and energy
2. Not being greedy
3. Generosity and unselfishness with time and resources
4. Contentment and joyfulness in any situation
5. Exercise of common sense
6. Not domineering over those who work under them
7. Having a life whose thoughts and actions are sexually pure

Students will show Christ's love for God and others. Some of the
attitudes and actions appropriate to this objective are:

1. Regularly setting goals which reflect the Great Commandment
2. Knowing and exercising correct priorities
3. Showing genuine and enduring love for others
4. An absence of bigotry and racism
5. Accepting others in spite of their differences or weaknesses

Students will demonstrate healthy attitudes and habits about work.
Some of the attitudes and actions appropriate to this objective are:

1. Ability to work hard without praise or recognition
2. Faithfulness in assuming and fulfilling assignments
3. Whole-hearted submission to authority; not stubborn or insub-
   ordinate
4. Healthy and positive attitudes about ministry
5. Knowing how to fail and still move forward; perseverance
6. Having a servant heart
7. Self-starting and motivating
8. Capable of independent action
9. Broad and open-minded thinking
10. Creativity in work; not merely imitative
11. Ability to live and work with ambiguities
12. Ability to focus on principles in a given situation rather than
    merely its particulars

CURRICULUM OF STUDIES
Conservative Baptist Seminary of the East

Diploma in Theology and Ministry

First Year

Course Title	Credits	Total
Fall Term		
Philosophy of Ministry	2	
Character Development Contract	1.5	
Doctrine of the Church	2	
Ministerial Skills Contract	1.5	
Greek Grammar	3	
		10
Winter Term		
Gospels	2	
Character Development Contract	1.5	
Hermeneutics and Cultural Adaption	3	
Dynamics of Christian Worship	2	
Ministerial Skills Contract	1.5	
		10

Spring Term

Foundations of the Gospel	3
Acts and Letters of Paul	2
Character Development Contract	1.5
Homiletics I	2
Ministerial Skills Contract	1.5
Integrative Seminar	1
	11

Second Year

Fall Term

Person and Work of Christ	2
Romans	2
Character Development Contract	1.5
Evangelism and Church Growth	3
Ministerial Skills Contract	1.5
	10

Winter Term

Work of the Holy Spirit	2
Character Development Contract	1.5
Homiletics II	2
World Vision	3
Ministerial Skills Contract	1.5
	10

Spring Term

Challenges to Christianity	2
Ministerial Skills Contract	1.5
History of Christianity I	2
Old Testament I	2
Character Development Contract	1.5
Introduction to the Hebrew Language I	1
Integrative Seminar	1
	11

Third Year

Fall Term

Topics from Hebrews through Revelation	2	
Character Development Contract	1.5	
Pastoral Counseling	2	
Ministerial Skills Contract	1.5	
Old Testament II	2	
Introduction to the Hebrew Language II	1	
		10

Winter Term

Church Administration	2	
Ministerial Skills Contract	1.5	
Old Testament III	2	
Character Development Contract	1.5	
Introduction to the Hebrew Language III	1	
Homiletics III	2	
		10

Spring Term

History of Christianity II	3	
Marriage, Family, and Friendship	2	
Ministerial Skills Contract	1.5	
Christianity and the Future	2	
Character Development Contract	1.5	
Integrative Seminar	1	
		11

TOTAL		93

ADULT EDUCATION PRINCIPLES AND PROCEDURES
A SELECT LIST OF READINGS

Apps, J.W.

1985   *Improving Practice in Continuing Education: Modern Approaches for Understanding the Field and Determining Priorities.* San Francisco: Jossey-Bass.

Brookfield, S.D.

1987   *Understanding and Facilitating Adult Learning.* San Francisco: Jossey-Bass.

Cross, P.

1981   *Adults as Learners: Increasing Participation and Facilitating Learning.* San Francisco: Jossey-Bass.

Daloz, L.

1987   *Effective Teaching as Mentoring.* San Francisco: Jossey-Bass.

Darkenwald, G.E., and S.B. Merriam.

1982   *Adult Education Foundations of Practice.* New York: Harper and Row.

Elias, J.L. and S.B. Merriam.

1980   *Philosophical Foundations of Adult Education.* Huntington, NY:
        Krieger.

Knowles, M.S.

1980   *The Modern Practice of Adult Education.* Revised. New York:
        Association Press.

Knox, A.B.

1986   *Helping Adults Learn.* San Francisco: Jossey-Bass.

Knox, A.B., and Associates.

1980   *Developing, Administering, and Evaluating Adult Education.* San
        Francisco: Jossey-Bass.

Tough, A.M., G. Griffin, B. Barnard, and D. Brundage.

1981   *The Design of Self-Directed Learning.* Toronto: Department of
        Adult Education, Ontario Institute for Studies in Education.

References and Endnotes

References

Chapters 1 and 2

Adeyemo, T.

1982   "The Renewal of Evangelical Theological Education." In Bowers,
         Evangelical Theological Education Today—II: Agenda for Renewal,
         pp. 5-12.

Bates, S.M., Baeta, C, Michaeli, F., and Sundkler, B.

1954   *Survey of the Training of the Ministry in Africa: Part II.* London:
         International Missionary Council.

Bergquist, J.A.

1973   "The TEF and the Uncertain Future of Third World Theological
         Education." *Theological Education*, 9, 4 (Summer), pp. 244-253.

Bowers, P. (ed.)

1982a   "Accreditation as a Catalyst for Renewal in Theological Educa-
         tion." In Bowers, *Evangelical Theological Education Today—II:
         Agenda for Renewal*, pp. 26-41.

1982b   *Evangelical Theological Education Today—I: An International Per-spective*. Nairobi: Evangel Publishing House.

1982c   *Evangelical Theological Education Today—I: Agenda for Renewal*. Nairobi: Evangel Publishing House.

Brown, W.A., and May, M.A.

1934   *The Education of American Ministers*. 4 vols. New York: Institute of Social and Religious Research.

Chow, W.

1982   "An Integrated Approach to Theological Education." In Bowers, *Evangelical Theological Education Today—I: An International Per-spective*, pp. 49-60

Coe, S.

1973   "In Search of Renewal in Theological Education." *Theological Education, 9*, 4 (Summer), pp. 233-243.

Conn, H.E.

1979   "Theological Education and the Search for Excellence." *West-minster Theological Journal, 51*, 2 (Spring), pp. 311-363.

Conn, H.E., and Rowen, S.F. (eds.)

1984   *Missions and Theological Education in World Perspective*. Farming-ton, MI: Associates of Urbanus.

Covell, R.R., and Wagner, C.P.

1971   *An Extension Seminary Primer*. South Pasadena, CA: William Carey Library.

Douglas, J. D. (ed.)

1975   Let the Earth Hear His Voice: *International Congress on World Evangelization, Lausanne, Switzerland*. Minneapolis, MN: World Wide Publications.

Farley, E.

1981   "The Reform of Theological Education as a Theological Task." *Theological Education, 17*, 2 (Spring), pp. 93-117.

1983   *Theologia: The Fragmentation and Unity of Theological Education*. Philadelphia: Fortress Press.

Ferris, R. W.

1986   "The Future of Theological Education." In Youngblood, Cyprus: *TEE Come of Age*, pp. 41-64.

1989   "Accreditation and TEE." In Youngblood, *Excellence and Renewal*, pp. 59-79.

Frame, J.

1984   "Proposals for a New North American Model." In Conn and Rowen, *Missions and Theological Education in World Perspective*. Farmington, MI: Associates of Urbanus, pp. 379-380.

Gnanakan, K.

1989   "Accreditation and Renewal." In Youngblood, *Excellence and Renewal: Goals for the Accreditation of Theological Education*, pp. 48-58.

Goodall, N., and Nielsen, E.W.

1954   *Survey of the Training of the Ministry in Africa: Part III*. London: International Missionary Council.

Hill, B.V.

1986   "Theological Education: Is It Out of Practice?" *Evangelical Review of Theology*, 10, 2 (April), pp. 174-182.

Hopewell, J.F.

1967   "Mission and Seminary Structure." *International Review of Missions*, 56 (April), pp. 158-163.

Hough, J.C., and Cobb, J.B.

1985   *Christian Identity and Theological Education.* Chico, CA: Scholars Press.

Howard, D.M.

1986   *The Dream that Would Not Die: The Birth and Growth of the World Evangelical Fellowship, 1846-1986.* Exeter, UK: The Paternoster Press.

Hulbert, T.

1989   "The Challenge of Renewal." In Youngblood, *Excellence and Renewal*, pp. 15-34.

Hwang, C.

1962   "A Rethinking of Theological Training for The Ministry in the Younger Churches Today." *South East Asia Journal of Theology*, 4, 2 (October), pp. 7-34.

International Council of Accrediting Agencies

1984   "Manifesto on the Renewal of Evangelical Theological Education." *Evangelical Review of Theology, 8,* 1 (April), pp. 136-143. Reprinted in Theological News, 16, 2 (April), 1984, pp. TET 1-6. Also reprinted in Youngblood, *Excellence and Renewal*, pp. 80-87.

International Missionary Council.

1939   *The Life of the Church*. Vol 4 in *The Madras Series* (7 vols). New York: International Missionary Council.

Lienemann-Perrin, C.

1981   *Training for a Relevant Ministry: A Study of the Contribution of the Theological Education Fund*. Geneva: The World Council of Churches.

McKinney, L.

1982a   "Serving the Church in Cultural Context: The Role of Academic Accreditation." In Bowers, *Evangelical Theological Education Today—I: An International Perspective*, pp. 34-48.

1982b   "Why Renewal is Needed in Theological Education." *Evangelical Missions Quarterly, 118*, 2 (April), pp. 85-96.

Neill, S.

1950   *Survey of the Training of the Ministry in Africa: Part I*. London: International Missionary Council.

Newbigin, L.

1978   "Theological Education in a World Perspective." *Ministerial Formation*, 4 (October), pp. 3-10. Reprinted in H.M. Conn and S.F. Rowen (eds.), *Missions and Theological Education in World Perspective*.

Nicholls, B.J.

1974   "Editorial: Means of Renewal." *Theological News, 6,* 4 (October-December), p. 1.

1975   "Theological Education and Evangelization." In J.D. Douglas (ed.), *Let the Earth Hear His Voice,* pp. 634-645.

1976   *Defending and Confirming the Gospel: The Report of the 1975 Consultation of the Theological Commission of the World Evangelical Fellowship.* New Delhi: WEF Theological Commission.

1982a   "Evangelical Theological Education in the Changing World of the 1980s." In Bowers, *Evangelical Theological Education Today—I: An International Perspective,* pp. 5-23.

1982b   "The Role of Spiritual Development in Theological Education." In Bowers, *Evangelical Theological Education Today—II: Agenda for Renewal,* pp. 13-25. Plueddemann, J.E.

1982   "Toward a Theology of Theological Education." In Bowers, *Evangelical Theological Education Today—II: Agenda for Renewal,* pp. 53-62.

1989   "The Challenge of Excellence." In Youngblood, *Excellence and Renewal,* pp. 1-14.

Niebuhr, H.R.

1956   *The Purpose of the Church and Its Ministry: Reflections on the Aims of Theological Education.* New York: Harper and Brothers.

Niebuhr, H.R., Williams, D.D., and Gustafson, J.M.

1957   *The Advancement of Theological Education.* New York: Harper and Brothers.

Ranson, C.W.

1946   *The Christian Minister in India: His Vocation and Training.* London:
        United Society for Christian Literature, Lutterworth Press.
        (First published in India, 1945.)

Ranson, C.W., Birkeli, F., Michaeli, F., and Rasendrahasina, T.

1957   *Survey of the Training of the Ministry in Madagascar.* London:
        International Missionary Council.

Ro, B.R.

1982   "Opportunities for International Cooperation in Evangelical
        Theological Education." In Bowers, *Evangelical Theological
        Education Today—I: An International Perspective,* pp. 24-33.

Scopes, W. (ed.)

1962   *The Christian Ministry in Latin America and the Caribbean.* Geneva:
        Commission on World Mission and Evangelism, World Coun-
        cil of Churches.

Solanky, A.D.

1978   "A Critical Evaluation of Theological Education in Residential
        Training." *Evangelical Review of Theology,* 2, 1 (April), pp. 124-
        133. Reprinted in H.M. Conn and S.F. Rowen, *Missions and
        Theological Education in World Perspective.*

Stackhouse, M.L.

1988   *Apologia: Contextualization, Globalization, and Mission in Theo-
        logical Education.* Grand Rapids: William B. Eerdmans Publish-
        ing Company.

Theological News.

1977a   "Asia Theological Association Finalises Accreditation Scheme."
         Theological News, 9, 2 (April), p. 4.

1977b   "Four Theological Schools Accepted as Registered Candidates
         for Accreditation." *Theological News, 9*, 3 (July), pp. 2-3.

1979a   "Accrediting Association Formed in the Caribbean." *Theological
         News, 11*, 2 (June), p. 5.

1979b   "Second European Evangelical Accreditation Conference Held
         in Switzerland." *Theological News, 11*, 2 (June), p. 5.

Tiènou, T.

1982   "Contextualization of Theology for Theological Education." In
         Bowers, *Evangelical Theological Education Today—II: Agenda for
         Renewal*, pp. 42-52.

Webster, D., and Nasir, K.L.

1962   *Survey of the Training of the Ministry in the Middle East.* Geneva:
         Commission on World Mission and Evangelism.

Winter, R.D. (ed.)

1969   *Theological Education by Extension.* South Pasadena, CA: William
         Carey Library

Youngblood, R.L. (ed.)

1986   Cyprus: *TEE Come of Age.* Exeter, UK: The Paternoster Press.

1989   *Excellence and Renewal: Goals for the Accreditation of Theological
         Education.* Exeter, UK: The Paternoster Press.

Endnotes

1. These papers were published in two anthologies edited by ICAA Executive Secretary, Robert Youngblood, *Cyprus: TEE Come of Age* (Exeter, UK: Paternoster Press, 1986) and *Excellence and Renewal: Goals for the Accreditation of Theological Education* (Exeter, UK: Paternoster Press, 1989).

2. I apologize for the obvious omission of schools in the Caribbean, Brazil, and Latin America from this list. The absence of Latin American representation in ICAA proved to be a major complication, although I received fine cooperation from CETA in the Caribbean. Ultimately, schools were selected from these areas for visits, but I was forced to cancel my planned visits due to limitations of time and funding. If this research can be extended, inclusion of those areas would certainly enrich the study.

3. Scheduling restrictions prevented me from completing this procedure at Bible College of South Australia (where my visit overlapped Anzac Day holidays) and at Tahlee Bible College (where I had only one day on campus). This was unfortunate since both of these colleges afford encouraging models for renewal. I still hope to publish descriptions of these programs in another forum.

4. The reader may also encounter calls for the "reform" of theological education. The terms appear to be used interchangeably in the literature, although "renewal" is the more common of the two.

5. Portions of this chapter were presented as a report to the International Council of Accrediting Agencies (ICAA) at its meeting in Wheaton, IL June 14-17, 1989, and published in *Evangelical Review of Theology, 14:1* (January 1990), pp. 64-77.

6. See Appendix B.

7. ICAA member agencies, as of June 1989, include:

Accrediting Council for Theological Education in Africa (ACTEA)
American Association of Bible Colleges (AABC)

Asia Theological Association (ATA)
Caribbean Evangelical Theological Association (CETA)
European Evangelical Theological Association (EETA)
South Pacific Association of Bible Colleges (SPABC)

8. See Appendix C. Because North American graduate theological schools are not represented among ICAA member agencies, the survey was broadened to include schools affiliated with the (North American) Fellowship of Evangelical Seminary Presidents. In recognition of the mutual agreement between Asia Theological Association (ATA) and the Philippine Association of Bible and Theological Schools (PABATS), furthermore, Philippine Bible colleges accredited by PABATS were included in the ATA sample.

Some areas of the world are conspicuously absent from the study, most notably Latin America. At this time no accrediting agency in Latin America is affiliated with ICAA (although a Brazilian association of evangelical theological schools, AETTE, is an associate member and has determined to launch an accrediting process). Efforts to establish contact with Latin American and other associations of evangelical theological schools have not been successful. The unrepresented areas clearly highlight a need to continue and extend this research. It is recognized that other fine evangelical institutions have not elected to seek accreditation by ICAA member agencies. The resulting deficiencies, however, do not threaten the validity of the research findings.

9. That is, when asked "Would you say you are familiar with the ICAA Manifesto?" the modal response was "somewhat familiar." Two agency leaders reported they are "very familiar" with the Manifesto, while three said they are "somewhat familiar," and one reported he is only "slightly familiar" with this document.

10. Some items were reported to be more common that others ("Integrated Programs" were relatively common—mean = 5.33; "Continuous Assessment" was reported to be rare—mean = 2.83). There were also significant differences among regional agencies (highest across twelve values = 5.00; lowest = 3.25). This may accurately reflect educational development in these regions, but variation among raters must be considered a strong rival hypothesis.

11. Bimodal patterns showed up in prioritization of "Spiritual Formation," "Holistic Curricularizing," "Christian Worldview," "Developmental Focus," and "A Cooperative Spirit."

12. Three agencies registered a relatively high negative correlation (Pearson's r = -.73 to -.88), but the other three agencies showed almost no correlation (r = .135 to -.129).

13. Mean response was 5.55 on a scale of 1 to 7 on which 1 = strongly disagree and 7 = strongly agree. It is noteworthy that 83.6% of respondents identified their opinion at points 5, 6, or 7 on the continuum.

14. Mean response was 4.95 on a 7 point scale with 1 = "Present Approach Serves Well" and 7 = "Major Change is Needed." Even though opinions were more distributed, 72.5% of respondents identified their position at points 5, 6, or 7 on the opinion scale.

15. Compare the ICAA agency respondents' mean "priority" response of 5.22 with institutional respondents' mean "importance" response of 6.23!

16. It is noteworthy that the largest discrepencies are seen in two values—"Outcomes Assessment" and "Creativity in Teaching"—and that these discrepencies exist across all seven agencies included in the study. It is evident that these are areas in which schools would appreciate help.

17. Responses varied from 48.0% identification of one or more other schools which demonstrate "Cultural Appropriateness," to only 17.5% identification of another school that demonstrates "Developmental Focus." Across all renewal values, furthermore, missing responses for this set of items was unusually high, ranging from 23% to 41%. If missing responses are not factored out, therefore, these data indicate even smaller ratios of educators able to identify schools which model renewal values.

18. *Canadian Theological Seminary Self Study: Part I—Report.* An unpublished report prepared by the Self Study Committee, Canadian Theological Seminary, Regina, Sasketchewan, May 1, 1988. Page 184.

19. *Canadian Theological Seminary Self Study: Part I—Report.* Unpublished report prepared by the Self Study Committee of Canadian Theological Seminary, Regina, Saskatchewan, May 1, 1988. Pages 186-187.

20. *Canadian Theological Seminary Self Study: Part 2—Appendices.* An unpublished report of the Self Study Committee of Canadian Theological Seminary, Regina, Sasketchewan, May 1, 1988. Appendix M—Self Study Outcomes Statistical Tables, p. M-30.

21. *Canadian Theological Seminary Self Study: Part I—Report.* An unpublished report of the Self Study Committee of Canadian Theological Seminary, Regina, Sasketchewan, May 1, 1988. Pages 177-178.

22. Following are the enrollment statistics in the Third Quarter, 1988-89:

Course	Part-Time	Full-Time
Diploma of Christian Studies	39	11
Master of Christian Studies	3	14
Master of Divinity	4	54
Master of Theology	9	0
TOTALS	55	79

23. Chapel is held on Tuesday, Thursday, and Friday mornings. Wednesday is reserved for faculty advisee group meetings.

24. It should be noted that Dip.C.S. students enrolled in the part-time, evening program are required to engage in a practicum which is essentially equivalent to the field education requirement for M.Div. and M.C.S. students.

25. During the summer of 1989, students will be going to East Malaysia and Pakistan, but in previous years other groups have been sent to Macau, Taiwan, Singapore, the Philippines, and Indonesia.

26. CGST refers to the evening extension school as theological education by extension (TEE). That terminology has been avoided in this report, since TEE tends to have very specific methodological associations (self study using programmed instructional texts and weekly small group discussions led by a facilitator) which do not hold in the extension program of CGST.

27. Evening extension courses offered during the Third Term 1988-89 included:

The Work of the Holy Spirit and Charismatic Gifts
Wisdom and Wisdom Literature in the Bible
Historic Figures of the Chinese Church
Studies in Systematic Theology: Ecclesiology, Sacraments and
    Eschatology
Presenting the Gospel in Commercial Areas
Pastoral Care and Evangelization of Terminal Patients
Renewal in Leading Corporate Worship

28. The term "basic stratum" refers to the majority of the Hong Kong population who enjoy very limited economic and educational benefits. The vast majority of the basic stratum are employed as factory workers or laborers in the transportation or food industries. The denotation is equivalent to other terms, such as "lower class" or "grassroots peoples," but carries no negative connotations.

29. Topics include the Christian's devotional life, personal discipline, life in the Spirit, and discovery and development of spiritual gifts.

30. Public seminars in recent years have focused on the themes, "Jesus, Who are You?" (1988—responding to the portrayal of Jesus in The Last Temptation of Christ), "Immigration" (1987—wrestling with issues of Christian responsibility and divine Lordship in national affairs in light of Hong Kong's reversion to the Peoples Republic of China in 1997), and "Do You Understand What You Read?" (using Philip's question in Acts 8 to clarify principles of Biblical hermeneutics).

31. A full description of the training programs of CBC and CBS is available from the institution and is beyond the scope of this study.

32. *Columbia Bible College, Academic Catalog 1988-89.* The catalog of the Seminary carries the same mission statement without the name of the institution.

33. Ralph E. Enlow, Ronald T. Habermas, Robert C. Kallgren, Nancy S. McCutcheon, Jay V. Sensenig, and Donald J. Trouten.

34. "Commission on the Future of the Bible College: Report and Recommendations." Unpublished report. Columbia Bible College. May, 1988.

35. Reference here to JETS as a "Bible college" reflects international usage. It may be of help to those unfamiliar with the African context to

understand how theological schools in Africa are commonly designated. It is not uncommon in Africa for "Bible school" to designate a theological school which operates at the primary or elementary school level. "Bible college" often refers to a secondary level training school for pastors and church workers. A post-secondary theological school is commonly designated a "seminary." In African context, therefore, it would not be accurate to refer to JETS as a "Bible College" as it appears here, and it is very appropriate for the school to carry the name "Jos ECWA Theological Seminary." From this point on, this case study will adopt African nomenclature.

36. Registration statistics for first term, 1988-89, indicate the following enrollment in degree programs:

Programs	1st Year	2nd Year	3rd Year	4th Year	Part Time	Thesis Ext.	PROG TOTAL
Pastoral Ministries	22	14	15	2	4	5	62
Teaching Ministries	9	5	10	1	1	6	32
Communications Minis.	2	0	1	1	0	1	5
TOTAL DEGREE STUDENTS							99

Distribution of students to the three basic majors, therefore, was:

Pastoral Studies	63%
Teaching the Bible	31%
Christian Communications	5%

37. In a recent study of JETS alumni and alumni from three other Nigerian seminaries, JETS appears to fare well vis a vis other institutions with respect to alumni opinion of their preparedness for ministry. See Paul J. Fritz, *An Evaluation of Evangelical Seminary Curricula for Teacher Training Effectiveness as it Applies in Nigeria* (dissertation for William Carey International University, Pasadena, CA), 1988.

38. When one member of the Brake faculty was asked what advice he would give to other theological schools desiring to improve their programs of training for ministry, his response was direct. Priority should be given to spiritual and mission education with as much academic instruction as can be given without jeopardizing the former. He went on to express the conviction that analytic disciplines do not contribute to spiritual thinking. While many may wish to debate this, two things are clear: this perspective is effectively implemented at Brake, and the results in the lives of Brake students are admirable.

39. The qualities employed in evaluating student character are: 1) Industry, 2) Initiative, 3) Responsibility, 4) Interpersonal relationships, 5) Emotional stability, and 6) Orderliness and appearance.

40. The camp schedule for 1989 was:

Senior Citizens Camp	May 31-June 13
Family Camp I	June 22-July 5
Family Camp II	July 7-26
Family Camp III	July 28-August 10
Family Camp IV	August 12-25

41. The schedule for a typical camp day includes a morning Bible teaching hour, personal and team sports competition, rest or quiet time, scheduled activities (e.g., family games, group outings or tours to places of historical interest, natural beauty, or public recreational parks), and an evening inspirational meeting, followed by free time until lights out at 11:00 p.m.

42. A different tutor is assigned at the beginning of the student's second year to guide his or her development during that year of study. Thus students in the two-year program have the opportunity to build a close relationship with two tutors. Two different tutors also have an opportunity to assess the strengths and needs of each student while addressing those needs in their own distinctive ways.

43. For a list of subjects in the two-year course, see Appendix D.

44. For examples of assignments listed for the 1988-89 academic year, see Appendix E.

45. All Nations Christian College is listed as the second largest among twenty-one Bible schools in Britain, according to a current brochure published by that nation's Association of Bible College Principals.

46. For the full UBS Bachelor of Divinity curriculum, see Appendix F.

47. For a statement of the goals of the internship year, see Appendix G.

48. For guidelines on preparing and discussing case studies, see Appendix H.

49. UBS Board Executive Committee minutes of December 19, 1971.

50. UBS Board of Governors minutes of March, 1975.

51. See Appendix I.

52. The thesis produced was: Pradip K. Das. *A Study of the Place of Training Programme of Union Biblical Seminary As Seen by Its Alumni.* A Bachelor of Divinity thesis. Yavatmal: Union Biblical Seminary, 1982.

53. Das, 1982, p. 63.

54. The article was subsequently published in *Evangelical Review of Theology*, *10*, 2 (April 1986), pp. 174-182.

55. Unpublished paper, n.d. See excerpts from the paper in Appendix J.

56. Originally published in *Ministerial Formation*, No. 10 (April 1980).

57. Board minutes 74-B-86 and 75-B-86 from the March 1986 meeting.

58. After the student submits a formal application, the Seminary addresses a letter to the student's home congregation which reads in part:

As a seminary serving the church, CBSE heeds the advice and counsel of the local assembly. For this reason, a letter from the church commending the applicant to us for training completes the admissions process.

The Seminary holds the conviction that God carries out His mission to a dying world through the local congregation and that the Seminary, directed and guided by that assembly of believers, provides the training. Would you kindly give the date when the church and the board convened to express their approval of the applicant for studies.

The response from the congregation becomes a part of the applicant's permanent file.

59. In cases where the student's home congregation is unable to provide an internship experience, the student must identify another congregation willing to assume this responsibility. A review of current students indicates that approximately 40% of students undertake their internship in a congregation other than their home church.

60. See Appendix K.

61. The CBSE curriculum is presented in Appendix L.

62. During the 1988-89 school year, semesters are reduced to fourteen weeks each term.

63. Matriculation of non-Conservative Baptist students is consistent with CBSE's stated commitment to serve Conservative Baptist churches and other congregations with similar commitments in theology and polity.

64. The Conservative Baptist Association of America organizes churches into three regional conferences, representing the Western states, the Mountain and Great Plains states (designated the Central Region), and the Eastern states. Denver Theological Seminary, founded in 1950, is located in the Central Region, and Western Theological Seminary, founded in 1927, is located in the Western Region. Until CBSE conducted its first class in September 1985, no Conservative Baptist seminary has existed in the East.

65. Atlanta: Southern Baptist Convention, 1978.

66. See Appendix M for a list of selected references on adult education principles and procedures.

67. More specific guidelines for preparing an outcomes study are included in the case study on Canadian Theological Seminary.

About the Author

Robert W. Ferris is a graduate of Wheaton College in Wheaton, Illinois (1961) with a degree in Bible. He also holds an M.A. degree in systematic theology from Wheaton College Graduate School, an M.Div. degree from Denver Conservative Baptist Seminary, and a Ph.D. in Curriculum Design from Michigan State University.

Dr. Ferris' wife, Sue, attended Wheaton College and earned a B.A. in biology. God dramatically led them to apply for a ministry in theological education under Far Eastern Gospel Crusade (now SEND International) in the Republic of the Philippines. They left the United States for Asia in May, 1967.

Bob Ferris served on the faculty of Febias College of Bible in Manila teaching New Testament, systematic theology, and related subjects for eight years. Between 1979 and 1988 he served concurrently as Executive Director of both the Philippine Association for Theological Education by Extension (PAFTEE) and the Philippine Association of Bible and Theological Schools (PABATS), and also as academic dean at Asian Theological Seminary in Manila. He has presented papers on theological education at several conferences in Asia and Europe including a major paper at the Cyprus consultation organized by World Evangelical Fellowship's International Council of Accrediting Agencies. In addition he was active in Asia Theological Association developing an accreditation program for TEE.

He has published articles in various journals such as *Theological News/Theological Education Today, Evangelical Review of Theology,* and *Christian Forum.*

Dr. Ferris feels God has called him to a ministry of reforming ministry training structures to make them more responsive to the needs of the church. He presently serves on the faculty of Columbia Biblical Seminary and Graduate School of Missions in Columbia, South Carolina.

Bob and Sue Ferris have two children, Rosalyn and Roger. Roger is a Bible and Philosophy major at Wheaton College. Rosalyn is a graduate of Wheaton and has already served the church abroad in Uganda, East Africa.